MUST-HAVE Grammar BOOK 2

HANILEDU.PUBLISHER

이 책의 특징

1 45개 필수 핵심 문법
- 9개의 공부법을 적용한 필수 핵심 문법으로 전권을 구성하였습니다.
- 문법, 글쓰기, 성적향상 그리고 영어 활용성을 동시에 해결할 수 있는 문법 순서와 내용으로 구성하였습니다.

2 KEY POINT 문법 설명
- 간결한 구성과 이해하기 쉬운 명쾌한 설명으로 구성하였습니다.
- 선생님과 학생들 모두 요점 이해와 파악이 쉽도록 꼭 필요한 POINT 설명만 담았습니다.

3 단계별 다양한 연습문제
- 배운 문법을 정확히 익히고 최대한 활용할 수 있도록 충분한 양의 연습문제를 제공하였습니다.
- 9개의 공부법 적용 : 단계별로 제시되는 다양한 연습문제를 통해 수업 집중도가 올라가고 문법 습득이 빨라집니다.

4 문법에서 쓰기까지 체계적 구성
- Grammar Point(문법 학습) → Grammar Exercise(연습문제) → Writing Practice(문장 및 문단쓰기) → Review(긴 문단쓰기)로 단계별 문법 연습과 쓰기 연습을 할 수 있습니다.

5 서술형, 논술형 평가 대비
- 다양한 쓰기, 단어, 읽기, 문법 문제를 통해 서술형과 논술형 수업과 시험을 체계적으로 대비할 수 있습니다.

6 장르별 영어 글쓰기
- 여러 가지 장르의 글을 통해 현장감 있는 영어를 배울 수 있도록 하였고, 사고력 확장에 도움을 줍니다.
- 편지글(Letter), 게시글(Notice), 리포트(Report), 에세이(Essay), 묘사하는 글쓰기(Descriptive essay), 연극 대본(Play script), 서사적 글쓰기(Narrative essay) 등과 같은 다양한 장르의 글이 포함되어 있습니다.

MUST-HAVE Grammar

구성과 특징

Part 1 Grammar Point

- 표 또는 수식을 활용하여, 문법 사항을 한 눈에 보기 쉽게 정리
- 명확한 핵심 문법 설명과 실용적인 예문

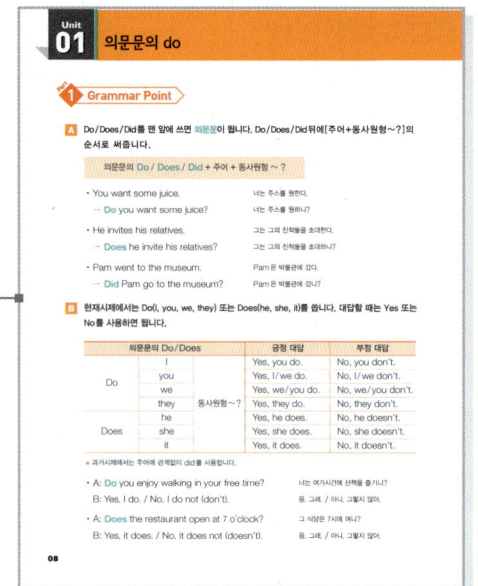
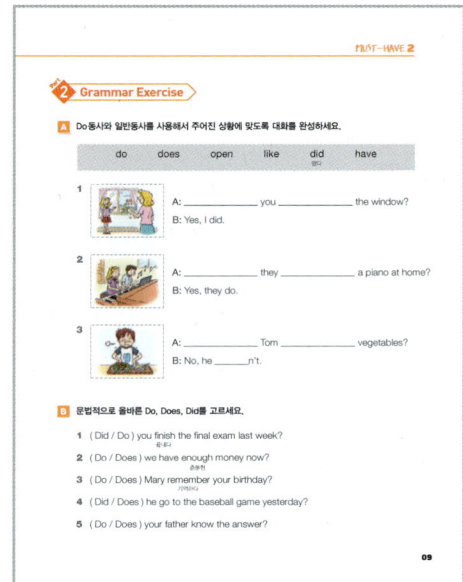
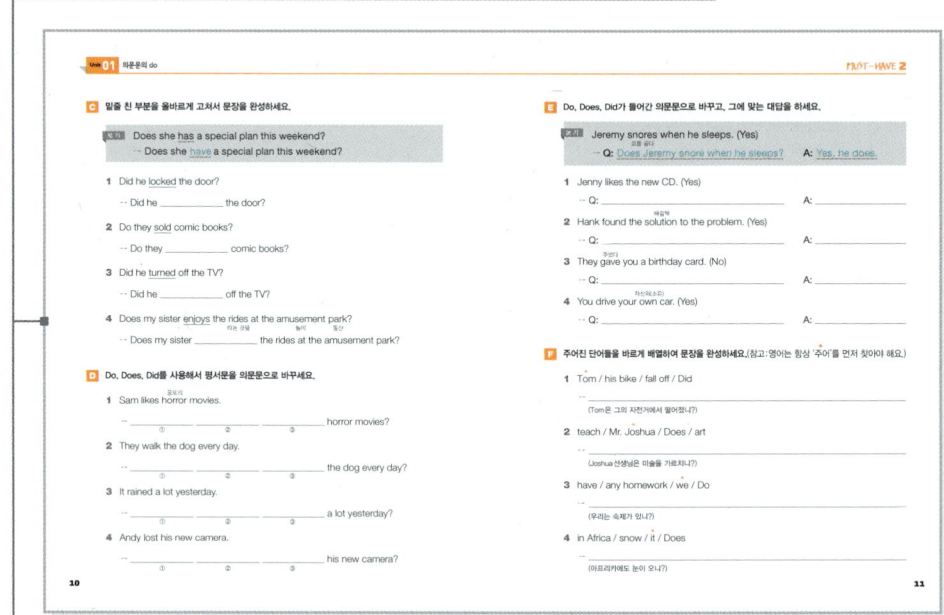

Part 2 Grammar Exercise

- 다양한 문법 연습문제를 단계별로 제시
- 핵심 문법의 체계적 연습

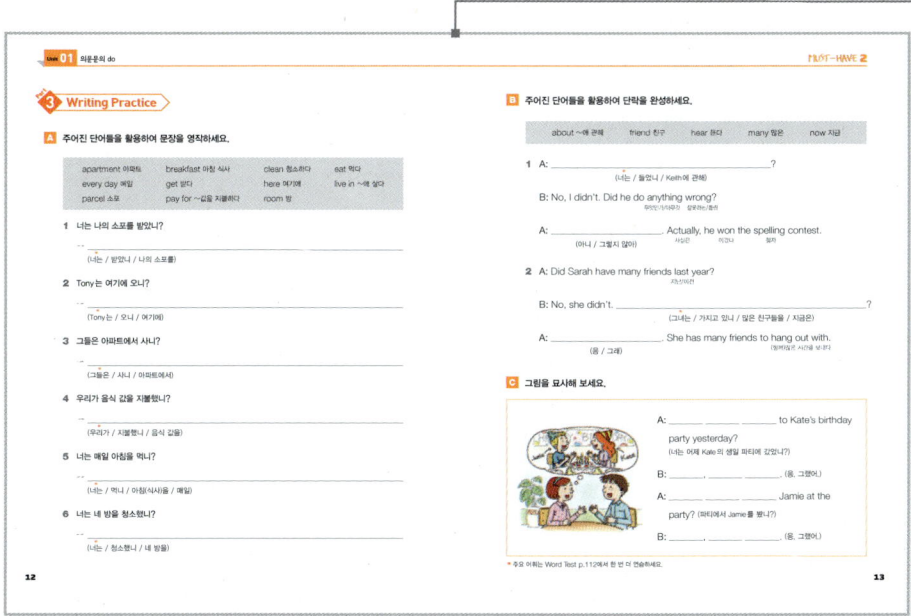

Part 3
Writing Practice

- 핵심 문법을 활용한 문장 및 짧은 단락 쓰기를 통해 글쓰기의 기초를 마련
- 다양한 쓰기 문제를 통해 서술형 평가 유형에 대비

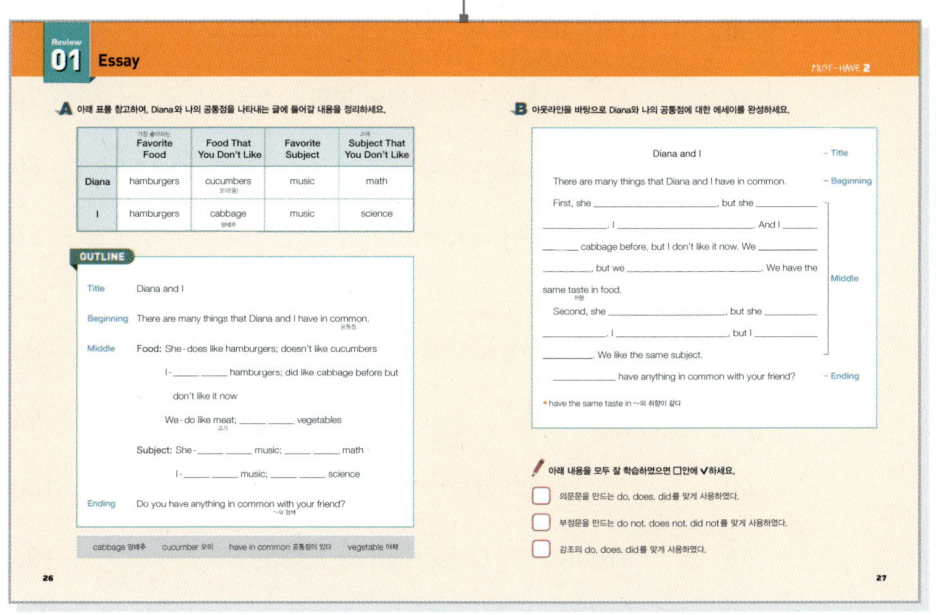

Review

- 핵심 문법을 적용한 완성된 글쓰기 연습
- 다양한 장르별 글쓰기 연습
- 글쓰기 후 핵심 문법 재확인

Appendix	불규칙 변화 동사표, to부정사를 목적어로 취하는 동사 모음
Word Test	Writing Practice에서 학습한 단어들을 점검해 볼 수 있는 단어 테스트
Answer Key	Unit별 연습문제와 Review의 정답

Contents MUST-HAVE Grammar

Book 2

1	의문문의 do	8
2	부정문의 do not	14
3	강조의 do	20

Review 1 Essay ... 26

4	인칭대명사	28
5	의문사가 있는 의문문	34
6	in order to / to	40

Review 2 Play Script ... 46

7	too ~ to / enough to	48
8	to부정사를 형용사처럼 쓰기	54
9	to부정사를 부사처럼 쓰기	60

Review 3 Essay ... 66

10	to부정사·동명사를 목적어로 쓰기	68
11	to부정사를 목적격 보어로 쓰기	74
12	-thing + 형용사	80

Review 4 Journal ... 86

13	과거분사 만들기	88
14	수동태	94
15	부정대명사	100

Review 5 Descriptive Essay ... 106

Appendix ... 108

Word Test ... 111

Answer Key ... 121

Book 1

1. 형용사 + 명사
2. 주어 + be동사 + 형용사
3. 명사의 단수와 복수, 관사

Review 1

4. 주어 + be동사 + 명사
5. 주어 + 일반동사 + 명사
6. 주어 + 동사 + 형용사 + 명사

Review 2

7. 전치사
8. 전치사구
9. 다수의 전치사구

Review 3

10. There is / There are
11. 부사; 형용사의 변형
12. 빈도부사

Review 4

13. 동명사
14. 현재분사
15. 현재진행형

Review 5

Appendix

Word Test

Answer Key

Book 3

1. 조동사의 형태
2. 미래의 조동사
3. 가능 · 추측 · 허가의 조동사

Review 1

4. 의무의 조동사
5. 습관의 조동사
6. 부사절을 만드는 접속사 1

Review 2

7. 부사절을 만드는 접속사 2
8. 수여동사
9. 지각동사와 사역동사

Review 3

10. 현재완료
11. 비교급
12. 수와 양을 나타내기

Review 4

13. 명사절
14. 형용사절
15. 복합관계사

Review 5

Appendix

Word Test

Answer Key

Unit 01 의문문의 do

Part 1 Grammar Point

A Do/Does/Did를 맨 앞에 쓰면 **의문문**이 됩니다. Do/Does/Did 뒤에 [주어+동사원형~?]의 순서로 써줍니다.

> 의문문의 Do / Does / Did + 주어 + 동사원형 ~ ?

- You want some juice.   너는 주스를 원한다.
  → **Do** you want some juice?   너는 주스를 원하니?

- He invites his relatives.   그는 그의 친척들을 초대한다.
  → **Does** he invite his relatives?   그는 그의 친척들을 초대하니?

- Pam went to the museum.   Pam은 박물관에 갔다.
  → **Did** Pam go to the museum?   Pam은 박물관에 갔니?

B 현재시제에서는 Do(I, you, we, they) 또는 Does(he, she, it)를 씁니다. 대답할 때는 Yes 또는 No를 사용하면 됩니다.

의문문의 Do/Does			긍정 대답	부정 대답
Do	I	동사원형~?	Yes, you do.	No, you don't.
	you		Yes, I/we do.	No, I/we don't.
	we		Yes, we/you do.	No, we/you don't.
	they		Yes, they do.	No, they don't.
Does	he		Yes, he does.	No, he doesn't.
	she		Yes, she does.	No, she doesn't.
	it		Yes, it does.	No, it doesn't.

* 과거시제에서는 주어에 관계없이 did를 사용합니다.

- A: **Do** you enjoy walking in your free time?   너는 여가시간에 산책을 즐기니?
  B: Yes, I do. / No, I do not (don't).   응, 그래. / 아니, 그렇지 않아.

- A: **Does** the restaurant open at 7 o'clock?   그 식당은 7시에 여니?
  B: Yes, it does. / No, it does not (doesn't).   응, 그래. / 아니, 그렇지 않아.

Part 2 Grammar Exercise

A Do동사와 일반동사를 사용해서 주어진 상황에 맞도록 대화를 완성하세요.

do	does	open	like	did	have
				했다	

1. A: _____ you _____ the window?
   B: Yes, I did.

2. A: _____ they _____ a piano at home?
   B: Yes, they do.

3. A: _____ Tom _____ vegetables?
   B: No, he _____n't.

B 문법적으로 올바른 Do, Does, Did를 고르세요.

1. (Did / Do) you finish the final exam last week?
   끝내다
2. (Do / Does) we have enough money now?
   충분한
3. (Do / Does) Mary remember your birthday?
   기억하다
4. (Did / Does) he go to the baseball game yesterday?
5. (Do / Does) your father know the answer?

Unit 01 의문문의 do

C 밑줄 친 부분을 올바르게 고쳐서 문장을 완성하세요.

> 보기 Does she <u>has</u> a special plan this weekend?
> → Does she have a special plan this weekend?

1 Did he <u>locked</u> the door?

→ Did he _____ the door?

2 Do they <u>sold</u> comic books?

→ Do they _____ comic books?

3 Did he <u>turned</u> off the TV?

→ Did he _____ off the TV?

4 Does my sister <u>enjoys</u> the rides at the amusement park?
   타는 것들   놀이   동산

→ Does my sister _____ the rides at the amusement park?

D Do, Does, Did를 사용해서 평서문을 의문문으로 바꾸세요.

1 Sam likes horror movies. (공포의)

→ _____ _____ _____ horror movies?
   ①   ②   ③

2 They walk the dog every day.

→ _____ _____ _____ the dog every day?
   ①   ②   ③

3 It rained a lot yesterday.

→ _____ _____ _____ a lot yesterday?
   ①   ②   ③

4 Andy lost his new camera.

→ _____ _____ _____ his new camera?
   ①   ②   ③

MUST-HAVE 2

E Do, Does, Did가 들어간 의문문으로 바꾸고, 그에 맞는 대답을 하세요.

> 보기   Jeremy snores when he sleeps. (Yes)
>   코를 골다
>   → Q: Does Jeremy snore when he sleeps?   A: Yes, he does.

1 Jenny likes the new CD. (Yes)

→ Q: _____   A: _____

           해결책
2 Hank found the solution to the problem. (Yes)

→ Q: _____   A: _____

      주었다
3 They gave you a birthday card. (No)

→ Q: _____   A: _____

              자신의(소유)
4 You drive your own car. (Yes)

→ Q: _____   A: _____

F 주어진 단어들을 바르게 배열하여 문장을 완성하세요.(참고:영어는 항상 '주어'를 먼저 찾아야 해요.)

1 Tom / his bike / fall off / Did

→ _____

(Tom은 그의 자전거에서 떨어졌니?)

2 teach / Mr. Joshua / Does / art

→ _____

(Joshua 선생님은 미술을 가르치니?)

3 have / any homework / we / Do

→ _____

(우리는 숙제가 있니?)

4 in Africa / snow / it / Does

→ _____

(아프리카에도 눈이 오니?)

Unit 01 의문문의 do

Part 3 Writing Practice

A 주어진 단어들을 활용하여 문장을 영작하세요.

apartment 아파트	breakfast 아침 식사	clean 청소하다	eat 먹다
every day 매일	get 받다	here 여기에	live in ~에 살다
parcel 소포	pay for ~값을 지불하다	room 방	

1 너는 나의 소포를 받았니?

→ _____

(너는 / 받았니 / 나의 소포를)

2 Tony는 여기에 오니?

→ _____

(Tony는 / 오니 / 여기에)

3 그들은 아파트에서 사니?

→ _____

(그들은 / 사니 / 아파트에서)

4 우리가 음식 값을 지불했니?

→ _____

(우리가 / 지불했니 / 음식 값을)

5 너는 매일 아침을 먹니?

→ _____

(너는 / 먹니 / 아침(식사)을 / 매일)

6 너는 네 방을 청소했니?

→ _____

(너는 / 청소했니 / 네 방을)

MUST-HAVE 2

B 주어진 단어들을 활용하여 단락을 완성하세요.

| about ~에 관해 | friend 친구 | hear 듣다 | many 많은 | now 지금 |

1 A: _____?
(너는 / 들었니 / Keith에 관해)

B: No, I didn't. Did he do anything wrong?
   무엇인가/아무것 잘못하는/틀린

A: _____. Actually, he won the spelling contest.
(아니 / 그렇지 않아)   사실은   이겼다   철자

2 A: Did Sarah have many friends last year?
                                지난/이전

B: No, she didn't. _____?
(그녀는 / 가지고 있니 / 많은 친구들을 / 지금은)

A: _____. She has many friends to hang out with.
(응 / 그래)   (함께 많은) 시간을 보내다

C 그림을 묘사해 보세요.

A: _____ _____ _____ to Kate's birthday party yesterday?
(너는 어제 Kate의 생일 파티에 갔었니?)

B: _____, _____ _____. (응, 그랬어.)

A: _____ _____ _____ Jamie at the party? (파티에서 Jamie를 봤니?)

B: _____, _____ _____. (응, 그랬어.)

* 주요 어휘는 Word Test p.112에서 한 번 더 연습하세요.

Unit 02 부정문의 do not

Part 1 Grammar Point

A do not / does not을 동사 앞에 쓰면 '일반동사의 부정문'이 됩니다. do not / does not의 과거형은 did not 한 가지만 있어요.

주어 + do / does / did + not + 동사원형

시제	인칭·수		형태
현재	1·2인칭, 복수형	I, you, we, they	do not (don't) + 동사원형
	3인칭 단수	he, she, it	does not (doesn't) + 동사원형
과거	모든 주어		did not (didn't) + 동사원형

- I like spinach. — 나는 시금치를 좋아한다.
  → I **do not** (**don't**) like spinach. — 나는 시금치를 좋아하지 않는다.

- You believe me. — 너는 나를 믿는다.
  → You **do not** (**don't**) believe me. — 너는 나를 믿지 않는다.

- She has a computer. — 그녀는 컴퓨터를 가지고 있다.
  → She **does not** (**doesn't**) have a computer. — 그녀는 컴퓨터를 가지고 있지 않다.

- The movie starts at 7. — 영화가 7시에 시작한다.
  → The movie **does not** (**doesn't**) start at 7. — 영화가 7시에 시작하지 않는다.

- Jim understood his parents. — Jim은 그의 부모님을 이해했다.
  → Jim **did not** (**didn't**) understand his parents. — Jim은 그의 부모님을 이해하지 못했다.

- They lent me a book. — 그들은 내게 책을 빌려주었다.
  → They **did not** (**didn't**) lend me a book. — 그들은 내게 책을 빌려주지 않았다.

Part 2 Grammar Exercise

A ① do동사의 부정 축약형을 만드세요.

do not → _____, does not → _____, did not → _____

② 주어진 상황을 완성하세요.

1. They _____ _____ lunch yesterday.
   do동사 (eat / ate) 점심

2. We _____ _____ to school on Saturdays.
   do동사 (goes / go)

3. He _____ _____ on the bed.
   do동사 (sleep / slept) 침대

B 문법적으로 올바른 don't, doesn't, didn't를 고르세요.

1. Heidi (don't / doesn't) go to the market on Sunday.

2. They (don't / doesn't) drink soft drinks.
   탄산음료수

3. The bell (don't / doesn't) ring after midnight.
   밤 12시

4. He (doesn't / didn't) go swimming last week.

5. I (didn't / don't) bring my umbrella this morning.
   가지고 오다

Unit 02 부정문의 do not

C 밑줄 친 부분을 올바르게 고쳐서 문장을 완성하세요.

> 보기 The sailors didn't fought on the ship.
> → The sailors didn't fight on the ship.

1 Jake doesn't knows the name of the plant. (행성)
 → Jake doesn't _____ the name of the plant.

2 The airplane didn't took off immediately.
 → The airplane didn't _____ off immediately. (즉시)

3 She didn't gives me her address. (주소)
 → She didn't _____ me her address.

4 They don't had any special plans. (특별한 계획들)
 → They don't _____ any special plans.

D 단어를 바르게 배열해서 문장을 완성하세요.

> 보기 We a math class don't have on Friday.
>   (③)   (①)   (②)

1 Emily sleep doesn't in class.
   ( )   ( )   ( )

2 I in Denver live don't.
   ( )   ( )   ( )

3 He speak doesn't English fluently. (유창하게)
   ( ) ( )   ( )

4 She didn't on a trip go to the island.
   ( )   ( )   ( )

E 부정문으로 바꿔 주세요. 꼭 축약형으로 작성하세요.

1. Kay helped the old lady.
   → Kay _____ _____ the old lady.

2. The man sells fresh fish. (신선한)
   → The man _____ _____ fresh fish.

3. They wear fancy clothes. (값비싼)
   → They _____ _____ fancy clothes.

4. Terry asks many questions in class. (질문들)
   → Terry _____ _____ many questions in class.

F 주어진 단어들을 바르게 배열하여 문장을 완성하세요.(참고:영어는 항상 '주어'를 먼저 찾아야 해요.)

1. did / wait for me / not / Tim
   → _____
   (Tim은 나를 기다리지 않았다.)

2. in the dormitory / don't / I / live
   → _____
   (나는 기숙사에 살지 않는다.)

3. speak clearly / not / She / does
   → _____
   (그녀는 명확하게 말하지 않는다.)

4. until 11 a.m. / The restaurant / open / doesn't
   → _____
   (그 식당은 오전 11시까지 열지 않는다.)

Unit 02 부정문의 do not

Part 3 Writing Practice

A 주어진 단어들을 활용하여 문장을 영작하세요.

at night 밤에	expensive 비싼	get in ~에 타다	gift 선물
go jogging 조깅하러 가다	in the sea 바다에서	miss 놓치다	on the weekend 주말에
swim 수영하다	today 오늘	want 원하다	watch 보다

1 Jeremy는 차에 타지 않았다.

→ _____

(Jeremy는 / 타지 않았다 / 차에)

2 나는 주말에는 조깅하러 가지 않는다.

→ _____

(나는 / 가지 않는다 / 조깅하러 / 주말에는)

3 나의 엄마는 밤에 TV를 보지 않는다.

→ _____

(나의 엄마는 / 보지 않는다 / TV를 / 밤에)

4 Sarah는 비싼 선물을 원하지 않는다.

→ _____

(Sarah는 / 원하지 않는다 / 비싼 선물을)

5 Naomi는 바다에서 수영하지 않았다.

→ _____

(Naomi는 / 수영하지 않았다 / 바다에서)

6 그는 오늘 학교 버스를 놓치지 않았다.

→ _____

(그는 / 놓치지 않았다 / 학교 버스를 / 오늘)

MUST-HAVE 2

B 주어진 단어들을 활용하여 단락을 완성하세요.

| a lot 많이 | cost 비용이 들다 | fight with ~와 싸우다 | junk food 인스턴트 음식 |
| lie 거짓말하다 | restaurant 식당 | serve 제공하다 | |

1 Trust is important between friends. _____.
   신뢰   중요한   ~ 사이에   (나는 / 거짓말하지 않는다 / 내 친구들에게)

   I also try to understand them. _____ either.
   ~ 하려고/~는것   이해하다   (나는 / 싸우지 않는다 / 그들과)

2 _____. The food is all
   (그 식당은 / 제공하지 않는다 / 인스턴트 음식을)

   healthy, and the service is excellent. Most of all, _____
   건강한   훌륭한/나무랄 데 없는   (그 식당은 / 비용이 들지 않는다 /

   _____.
   많이)

C 그림을 묘사해 보세요.

It _____ _____ in the Sahara Desert.
(사하라 사막에는 눈이 오지 않는다.)

People there _____ _____ short sleeves. (그곳 사람들은 반팔 옷을 입지 않는다.)

They _____ _____ barefoot.
(그들은 맨발로 걷지 않는다.)

They _____ _____ pork.
(그들은 돼지고기를 먹지 않는다.)

* 주요 어휘는 Word Test p.112에서 한 번 더 연습하세요.

Unit 03 강조의 do

Part 1 Grammar Point

A 동사의 의미를 **강조**하려면 그 동사 앞에 do/does/did를 쓰면 됩니다. do/does/did 뒤에는 항상 동사원형을 씁니다.

> 강조의 **do** / **does** / **did** + 동사원형: 정말(꼭) ~하다

- I like comics. / 나는 만화책을 좋아한다.
  → I **do** like comics. / 나는 만화책을 정말 좋아한다.
- Gary knows how to get to the station. / Gary는 역까지 가는 방법을 알고 있다.
  → Gary **does** know how to get to the station. / Gary는 역까지 가는 방법을 정말 알고 있다.
- He came home right after school. / 그는 학교 끝나고 곧장 집에 왔다.
  → He **did** come home right after school. / 그는 학교 끝나고 정말 곧장 집에 왔다.

B 현재시제에서는 do 또는 does를 쓰고, 과거시제에서는 did를 씁니다.

시제	인칭·수		형태
현재	1·2인칭, 복수형	I, you, we, they	do + 동사원형
	3인칭 단수	he, she, it	does + 동사원형
과거	모든 주어		did + 동사원형

- I **do** like loud music. / 나는 시끄러운 음악을 정말 좋아한다.
- They **do** have problems. / 그들은 정말 문제가 있다.
- Jane **does** feel dizzy today. / Jane은 오늘 정말 어지럽다.
- My mother **does** enjoy cooking for us. / 나의 엄마는 우리를 위해 요리하는 것을 정말 즐긴다.
- He **did** win the contest. / 그는 대회에서 정말 우승을 했다.
- We **did** have a good time at the party. / 우리는 파티에서 정말 좋은 시간을 보냈다.

Part 2 Grammar Exercise

A 강조의 do, does, did를 사용해서 주어진 상황을 '강조'해서 설명해 주세요.

| look | does | brush 닦다 | do | did | smell 냄새(향)가 나다 |

1. You _____ _____ great in the blue shirt today.

2. This flower _____ _____ good.

3. I _____ _____ my teeth this morning.

B 문법적으로 올바른 강조의 do 동사를 고르세요.

1. We (do / does) hope to see you again.
   희망하다   다시

2. He (do / does) want to be a singer.

3. They (do / did) solve the problem yesterday.
   풀다

4. My father (does / did) wash the dishes last weekend.
   설거지하다

5. I (do / does) learn a lot from books.

Unit 03 강조의 do

C 밑줄 친 단어가 강조하는 말을 찾아 동그라미 하세요.

> 보기 Kay does (enjoy) taking a walk in the evening.

1 They did wash their car in the morning.

2 I do go swimming every weekend.

3 Her brother does want to be a manager.
관리자

4 We did find the way to the hotel.

5 He does look nervous in front of people.
긴장한

D 밑줄 친 부분을 올바르게 고쳐서 문장을 완성하세요.

> 보기 Dr. Anderson does takes care of poor people.
> → Dr. Anderson does take care of poor people.

중요한   결정
1 Tony did made an important decision.

→ Tony did _____ an important decision.

흥미있는
2 Amy does has an interesting hobby.

→ Amy does _____ an interesting hobby.

심하게
3 It did rained heavily last night.

→ It did _____ heavily last night.

4 I do liked my hairstyle.

→ I do _____ my hairstyle.

약
5 Mom did took medicine after breakfast.

→ Mom did _____ medicine after breakfast.

E 강조의 do동사를 사용해서 이 문장들을 모두 강조해 주세요.

1 I study a lot before the exam. (~전에)
   → _____

2 The child sleeps alone every night. (혼자)
   → _____

3 He came to school yesterday.
   → _____

4 Nancy speaks French fluently.
   → _____

5 My sister made pasta for me.
   → _____

F 주어진 단어들을 바르게 배열하여 문장을 완성하세요. (참고: 영어는 항상 '주어'를 먼저 찾아야 해요.)

1 go / I / did / to the hospital
   → _____
   (나는 그 병원에 정말 갔다.)

2 have / does / special talents / Jack
   → _____
   (Jack은 특별한 재능들을 정말 갖고 있다.)

3 know / We / do / the truth
   → _____
   (우리는 진실을 정말 알고 있다.)

4 did / on the playground / run a lot / They
   → _____
   (그들은 운동장에서 정말 많이 달렸다.)

Unit 03 강조의 do

Part 3 Writing Practice

A 주어진 단어들을 활용하여 문장을 영작하세요.

enough 충분한	have 가지다	loud 소리가 큰	machine 기계
make 만들다	make a mistake 실수를 하다	new 새로운	on Saturdays 토요일마다
phone number 전화번호	remember 기억하다	take a walk 산책하다	uncle 삼촌
voice 목소리			

1 나는 토요일마다 꼭 산책한다.
→ _____
   (나는 / 꼭 / 산책한다 / 토요일마다)

2 너의 삼촌은 정말 큰 목소리를 가지고 있다.
→ _____
   (너의 삼촌은 / 정말 / 가지고 있다 / 큰 목소리를)

3 나는 정말 너의 전화번호를 기억한다.
→ _____
   (나는 / 정말 / 기억한다 / 너의 전화번호를)

4 Lenny는 정말 큰 실수를 했다.
→ _____
   (Lenny는 / 정말 / 큰 실수를 했다)

5 우리는 정말 충분한 시간을 가지고 있다.
→ _____
   (우리는 / 정말 / 가지고 있다 / 충분한 / 시간을)

6 James는 새로운 기계를 정말 만들었다.
→ _____
   (James는 / 정말 / 만들었다 / 새로운 / 기계를)

B 주어진 단어들을 활용하여 단락을 완성하세요.

| air 공기 | care for ~을 보살피다 | clean 깨끗한 | fresh 신선한 |
| give 주다 | like 좋아하다 | rain 비 | rainy day 비오는 날 |

1 It is raining heavily. Some people don't like rainy days. But _____
   억수같이/심하게/많이   (나는 / 정말 / 좋아한다 /

_____. _____
   비오는 날을)   (비는 / 정말 / 준다 / 우리에게 / 깨끗하고 신선한 /

_____.
   공기를)

2 John and I went to the same elementary school. And _____
              같은   (우리는 / 정말 / 가졌다 /

_____. John was like my elder brother. _____
   좋은 시간을)   나이가 더 많은   (그는 / 정말 / 보살펴 주었다 /

_____.
   나를)

C 그림을 묘사해 보세요.

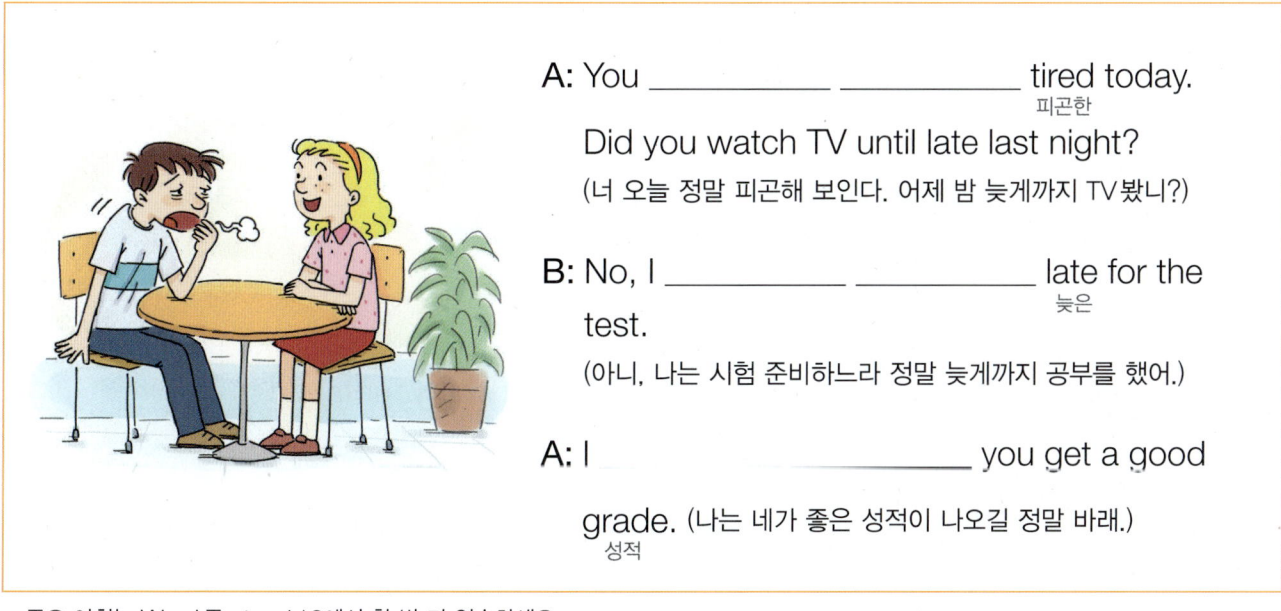

A: You _____ _____ tired today.
                              피곤한
Did you watch TV until late last night?
(너 오늘 정말 피곤해 보인다. 어제 밤 늦게까지 TV 봤니?)

B: No, I _____ _____ late for the
                              늦은
test.
(아니, 나는 시험 준비하느라 정말 늦게까지 공부를 했어.)

A: I _____ you get a good

grade. (나는 네가 좋은 성적이 나오길 정말 바래.)
   성적

* 주요 어휘는 Word Test p.113에서 한 번 더 연습하세요.

Review 01 Essay

A 아래 표를 참고하여, Diana와 나의 공통점을 나타내는 글에 들어갈 내용을 정리하세요.

	가장 좋아하는 Favorite Food	Food That You Don't Like	Favorite Subject	과목 Subject That You Don't Like
Diana	hamburgers	cucumbers 오이(들)	music	math
I	hamburgers	cabbage 양배추	music	science

OUTLINE

Title Diana and I

Beginning There are many things that Diana and I have in common. 공통점

Middle Food: She - does like hamburgers; doesn't like cucumbers

I - _____ _____ hamburgers; did like cabbage before but don't like it now

We - do like meat; _____ _____ vegetables
고기

Subject: She - _____ _____ music; _____ _____ math

I - _____ _____ music; _____ _____ science

Ending Do you have anything in common with your friend?
~와 함께

---

cabbage 양배추   cucumber 오이   have in common 공통점이 있다   vegetable 야채

B 아웃라인을 바탕으로 Diana와 나의 공통점에 대한 에세이를 완성하세요.

Diana and I — Title

There are many things that Diana and I have in common. — Beginning

First, she _____, but she _____
_____. I _____. And I _____
_____ cabbage before, but I don't like it now. We _____
_____, but we _____. We have the
same taste in food.
　　　　　취향
　　Second, she _____, but she _____
_____. I _____, but I _____
_____. We like the same subject.

_____ have anything in common with your friend? — Ending

* have the same taste in ~의 취향이 같다

— Middle

아래 내용을 모두 잘 학습하였으면 □안에 ✓하세요.

☐ 의문문을 만드는 do, does, did를 맞게 사용하였다.

☐ 부정문을 만드는 do not, does not, did not를 맞게 사용하였다.

☐ 강조의 do, does, did를 맞게 사용하였다.

Unit 04 인칭대명사

Part 1 Grammar Point

A 어떤 명사를 대신해서 쓴 말을 대명사라고 합니다. 사람 또는 사물을 대신해서 쓴 대명사를 **인칭대명사**라고 해요.

인칭대명사			
주격(주어 역할) (~은/는)	소유격 (~의)	목적격(목적어 역할) (~에게, ~을/를)	소유대명사 (~의 것)
I	my	me	mine
you	your	you	yours
he	his	him	his
she	her	her	hers
it	its	it	–
we	our	us	ours
they	their	them	theirs

- Jane loves Tom very much.
  = **She** loves **him** very much. 그녀는 그를 아주 많이 사랑한다.

- Tony and Mike didn't invite Susie and me.
  = **They** didn't invite **us**. 그들은 우리를 초대하지 않았다.

- Cathy sent a postcard to Ken and Scott.
  = **She** sent a postcard to **them**. 그녀는 그들에게 엽서를 보냈다.

- Mary and I bought apples from Ms. White.
  = **We** bought apples from **her**. 우리는 그녀에게서 사과를 샀다.

- The phone is **my** phone. = The phone is **mine**. 그 전화기는 나의 것이다.

- Greg took **his** coat, and Janet took **hers**. Greg는 그의 코트를 가져갔고, Janet은
                                    = her coat   그녀의 것을 가져갔다.

* Tony's car (Tony의 자동차)에서 Tony's (Tony의 것)를 '소유대명사'라고 합니다.

Part 2 Grammar Exercise

A ① 인칭대명사를 주격 (☆), 소유격(△), 목적격(○)으로 표시하세요.

| his | him | she | they |

② 주어진 상황을 설명하세요

1  Frank washed _____ car yesterday.
씻었다

2  The girls are Kim and Tammy. _____ are good friends.

3  Nick is Rosa's best friend. _____ calls _____ almost every day.
거의

B 대명사의 사용이 올바른 것을 고르세요.

1 Fred wants to return (she / her / hers) book to her.
돌려주다

2 (Us / Our / We) should take care of our planet.
소중히 하다

3 George saw (his / he / him) face in the mirror.

4 Don't use my computer. Use (you / your / yours).

5 Ann asked (my / me / I) to buy some milk.
부탁했다

Unit 04 인칭대명사

C 밑줄 친 대명사를 문맥에 맞게 고쳐 쓰세요.

> 보기 Gary showed me the price of he jacket.
> 보여주었다   가격
> → Gary showed me the price of his jacket.

1 Pam doesn't have she student ID.
   학생증
   → Pam doesn't have _____ student ID.

2 My father wanted me to help he.
   → My father wanted me to help _____.

3 David and Jenny don't know whether the car is they.
   ~인지 아닌지
   → David and Jenny don't know whether the car is _____.

D 밑줄 친 부분을 알맞은 대명사로 바꾸어 문장을 완성하세요.

> 보기 Kevin is doing Kevin's homework.
> → He is doing his homework.

1 My brother and I found Susie and Olive at the park.
   찾았다
   → _____ found _____ at the park.

2 Ted brought his diary, and Lisa brought her diary.
   가지고 왔다
   → _____ brought his, and _____ brought _____.

3 Your house is big, but I think their house is bigger.
                                              더 큰
   → Your house is big, but I think _____ is bigger.

4 David did the history project with Jane and me.
                                  역사
   → _____ did the history project with _____.

E 내용상 적절한 인칭대명사를 고르세요.

1. Q: Are (their / theirs) answers correct?
   　　　　　　　　　　답들　　　정확한
   A: No, they aren't. (Our / Ours) are correct.

2. Q: Do you know (him / his) phone number?
   A: No, I don't know (it / its).

3. Q: Is this (your / yours) book?
   A: Yes, that's (my / mine).

4. Q: Is Mary sitting in (her / hers) seat?
   　　　　　　　　　　　　　　　　　　의자
   A: No, she is sitting in (Jake / Jake's).

F 주어진 단어들을 바르게 배열하여 문장을 완성하세요.(참고:영어는 항상 '주어'를 먼저 찾아야 해요.)

1. I / with them / talking / enjoy

   → _____

   (나는 그들과 이야기하는 것을 즐긴다.)

   　이해하다
2. understand / We / didn't / her idea

   → _____

   (우리는 그녀의 생각을 이해하지 못했다.)

3. these shoes / I think / his / are

   → _____

   (나는 이 신발이 그의 것이라고 생각한다.)

   　　　　　　서다
4. told / He / to stand by her / me

   → _____

   (그는 내게 그녀 옆에 서라고 말했다.)

Unit 04 인칭대명사

Part 3 Writing Practice

A 주어진 단어들을 활용하여 문장을 영작하세요.

announce 발표하다	call 부르다	can't ~할 수 없다	future 미래
hero 영웅	just 방금	part 부분	purse (여성용) 지갑
read 읽다	return 돌아오다	rule 규칙	school 학교
tell 알다, 분간하다	think 생각하다	trip 여행	

1 그는 자신의 아빠를 영웅이라고 부른다.
→ _____
(그는 / 부른다 / 자신의 아빠를 / 영웅이라고)

2 나는 그 지갑이 그녀의 것이라고 생각한다.
→ _____
(나는 / 생각한다 / 그 지갑이 / 이다 / 그녀의 것이라고)

3 Nick은 그의 부분을 읽었고, 나는 내 것을 읽었다
→ _____
(Nick은 / 읽었다 / 그의 부분을 / 그리고 / 나는 / 읽었다 / 내 것을)

4 우리는 우리의 미래를 알 수 없다.
→ _____
(우리는 / 알 수 없다 / 우리의 미래를)

5 Mike는 그의 여행에서 방금 돌아왔다.
→ _____
(Mike는 / 방금 / 돌아왔다 / 그의 여행에서)

6 그는 우리에게 새로운 학교 규칙을 발표했다.
→ _____
(그는 / 발표했다 / 새로운 / 학교 규칙을 / 우리에게)

B 주어진 단어들을 활용하여 단락을 완성하세요.

| best 가장 좋은 | birthday 생일 | buy 사다 | friend 친구 |
| next 다음의 | play soccer 축구를 하다 | wait for ~을 기다리다 | |

1 I want to have the cell phone. But _____
(나의 엄마는 / 사주지 않는다 / 그것을 /

_____. She thinks I don't need it now. But she promises me to buy
나를 위해서)   약속하다

it next year. So _____.
(나는 / 기다리고 있다 / 나의 다음 생일을)

2 _____. _____
(Gary는 / 이다 / 나의 가장 좋은 / 친구)   (나는 / 축구를 한다 /

_____ after school. We sometimes play until late at night.
그와 함께)   ~ 때 까지

C 그림을 묘사해 보세요.

A: Did _____ bring _____ notebook?
(너의 공책을 가져왔니?)

B: Yes, I brought _____ here.
(네, 여기 그것(공책)을 가져왔어요.)

A: _____ want _____ to write a short essay. (나는 네가 짧은 글쓰기를 했으면 좋겠다.)

B: Okay. But can _____ borrow _____ _____?
(좋아요. 그런데 제가 선생님의 연필을 빌릴 수 있을까요?)

* 주요 어휘는 Word Test p.113에서 한 번 더 연습하세요.

Unit 05 의문사가 있는 의문문

Part 1 Grammar Point

A '6개의 의문사'를 문장 맨 앞에 써주면 의문문이 됩니다. 문장 속에는 반드시 주어와 동사가 있어야 합니다.

종류	who(m) 누가(누구를)	why 왜	when 언제	what 무엇	where 어디	how 어떻게
형태	• 의문사 + be동사 + 주어 ~ ? • 의문사 + 조동사 + 주어 + 동사원형 ~ ? • 의문사 + do/does/did + 주어 + 동사원형 ~ ?					

- A: **When** is your birthday? 너는 생일이 언제니?
  B: It's on May 2. 5월 2일이야.

- A: **Who** is that man? 저 사람은 누구니?
  B: He is my English teacher. 그는 나의 영어 선생님이야.

- A: **How** can you forget my name? 어떻게 내 이름을 잊어버릴 수 있니?
  B: I am so sorry. 정말 미안해.

- A: **What** did you choose? 너는 무엇을 골랐니?
  B: I chose the pink shirt. 나는 핑크색 셔츠를 골랐어.

- A: **Where** does she go? 그녀는 어디에 가니?
  B: She goes to the gym. 그녀는 체육관에 가.

- A: **Why** did you turn on the light? 너는 왜 불을 켰니?
  B: It was dark in here. 여기가 어두웠어.

- A: **Who(m)** did you meet yesterday? 어제 너는 누구를 만났니?
  B: I met Jack. 나는 Jack을 만났어.

Part 2 Grammar Exercise

A 주어진 상황에 맞는 의문사를 골라 문장을 완성하세요.

| who | what | why |

1
A: _____ are you so sad?
　　　　　　　　　　슬픈
B: I lost my watch.
　　잃어버렸다

2
A: _____ did you see last night?
B: I saw the fireworks with my parents.
　　　　불꽃놀이

3
A: _____ is your favorite actor?
B: My favorite actor is Ryan Gosling.

B 내용상 가장 적절한 의문사를 고르세요.

1 (Where / What) is my colored pencil?
　　　　　　　　　　　색　　연필

2 (What / How) did John talk about?

3 (Whom / How) did you come here?

4 (Who / Where) does Dan live in Korea?

5 (When / Why) can you finish the paper?
　　　　　　　　　끝내다　　보고서/작문 숙제

Unit 05 의문사가 있는 의문문

C 밑줄 친 부분을 올바르게 고쳐서 문장을 완성하세요.

1 Whom did Martin <u>invites</u> to the meeting? (초대하다)

   → Whom did Martin _____ to the meeting?

2 Where did Jim <u>played</u> baseball?

   → Where did Jim _____ baseball?

3 What can you <u>told</u> me about it?

   → What can you _____ me about it?

4 When does she <u>goes</u> to bed?

   → When does she _____ to bed?

D 주어진 대답(B:)이 나오기 위해서 어떻게 물어야 할까요? 알맞은 의문사를 사용해서 문장을 완성하세요.

1 A: _____ did you buy at the mall?

   B: I bought a skirt. (샀다)

2 A: _____ was the weather yesterday? (날씨)

   B: It was cloudy and windy. (구름이 낀)

3 A: _____ joined the club? (클럽/동호회)

   B: Naomi and Pam did.

4 A: _____ does the ballet start? (발레)

   B: It starts at 5 p.m.

5 A: _____ do you know her?

   B: She is Lenny's classmate.

E 밑줄 친 단어를 올바르게 배열해서 의문문을 완성하세요.

> 보기 did   What   you   do   on Christmas Eve?
>   (②)   (①)   (③) (④)

1 were   Where   you   last   weekend?
   (   ) (   )   (   )

2 Why   go   she   did   to   Canada?
   ( ) ( ) ( ) ( )

3 did   Whom   they   elect   as   class   president?
   ( ) ( )   ( )   ( )   회장/반장

4 we   can   finish   When   the   discussion?
   ( ) ( ) ( )   ( )   회의

F 주어진 단어들을 바르게 배열하여 문장을 완성하세요.(참고:영어는 항상 '주어'를 먼저 찾아야 해요.)

1 next taekwondo lesson / is / When / your

   → _____

   (너의 다음 태권도 강습은 언제니?)

2 so late / you / Why / are

   → _____

   (왜 이렇게 늦었니?)

3 play soccer / do / Where / you

   → _____

   (너는 어디서 축구를 하니?)

4 did / What / last Sunday / you do

   → _____

   (지난 일요일에 뭐했니?)

Unit 05 의문사가 있는 의문문

Part 3 Writing Practice

A 주어진 단어들을 활용하여 문장을 영작하세요.

buy 사다	dinner 저녁 식사	eat 먹다	experiment 실험
match 시합	nervous 불안한	so 그렇게, 너무	start 시작하다
tennis 테니스	ticket 표	win 이기다	yesterday 어제

1 왜 그들은 그렇게 불안해하니?

→ _____

(왜 / 그들은 / 그렇게 / 불안해하니)

2 너는 어디에서 그 표를 샀니?

→ _____

(어디에서 / 너는 / 샀니 / 그 표를)

3 David는 언제 저녁을 먹니?

→ _____

(언제 / David는 / 먹니 / 저녁(식사)을)

4 그녀는 어제 누구를 봤니?

→ _____

(누구를 / 그녀는 / 봤니 / 어제)

5 너는 그 실험을 언제 시작하니?

→ _____

(언제 / 너는 / 시작하니 / 그 실험을)

6 그녀는 어떻게 테니스 시합에서 이겼니?

→ _____

(어떻게 / 그녀는 / 이겼니 / 테니스 시합에서)

B 주어진 단어들을 활용하여 단락을 완성하세요.

> ask 묻다 can ~할 수 있다 last weekend 지난 주말 parent (복수로) 부모님
> what should ~ ? 무엇을 해야 할까

1. A: _____?
   (어디에 / Mary는 / 갔니 / 지난 주말에)
   B: She went to church. _____?
   (왜 / 너는 / 묻니)
   A: I want to find out something from her.
   알아내다

2. A: _____?
   (무엇을 해야 할까? / 나는 / 사다 / 나의 부모님을 위해서)
   B: I think flowers will be good.

   A: _____ some flowers?
   (어디서 / 할 수 있나 / 내가 / 사다)
   B: There is a flower shop on the next block.
   ~이 있다

C 그림을 묘사해 보세요.

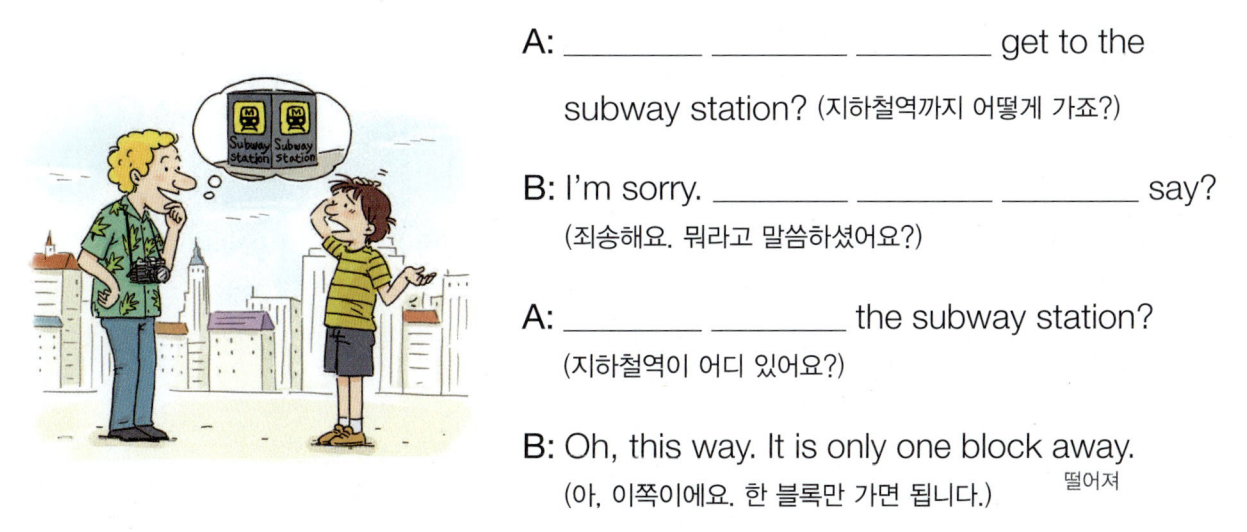

A: _____ _____ _____ get to the subway station? (지하철역까지 어떻게 가죠?)

B: I'm sorry. _____ _____ _____ say?
(죄송해요. 뭐라고 말씀하셨어요?)

A: _____ _____ the subway station?
(지하철역이 어디 있어요?)

B: Oh, this way. It is only one block away.
(아, 이쪽이에요. 한 블록만 가면 됩니다.) 떨어져

* 주요 어휘는 Word Test p.114에서 한 번 더 연습하세요.

Unit 06 in order to / to

Part 1 Grammar Point

A [in order to / to]는 '~하기 위하여'라는 목적과 의도를 나타냅니다.

> **in order to / to + 동사원형: ~하기 위하여**

- Susan visited the town **in order to** see her grandparents.
  = Susan visited the town **to** see her grandparents.
  Susan은 자신의 조부모님을 뵙기 위해 그 마을을 방문했다.

- People wear boots **in order to** keep their feet warm and dry.
  = People wear boots **to** keep their feet warm and dry.
  사람들은 자신의 발을 따뜻하고 물기 없게 하기 위해서 부츠를 신는다.

B [in order to / to] 뒤에는 반드시 동사원형을 써주세요.

- Gary went jogging to was healthy. (X)
  → Gary went jogging to be healthy.   Gary는 건강해지기 위해 조깅하러 갔다.

- Peter studies hard in order to gets good grades. (X)
  → Peter studies hard in order to get good grades.   Peter는 좋은 점수를 받기 위해 열심히 공부한다.

C [in order to / to] 문장의 부정형은 to 앞에 not을 붙이면 됩니다.

> **in order not to / not to + 동사원형: ~하지 않기 위하여**

- Jane tried her best **in order not to** fail.   Jane은 실패하지 않기 위해서 최선을 다했다.
  = Jane tried her best **not to** fail.

- They ran fast **in order not to** miss the train.   그들은 기차를 놓치지 않기 위해서 빨리 뛰었다.
  = They ran fast **not to** miss the train.

MUST-HAVE 2

Part 2 Grammar Exercise

A ① 동사를 [to + 동사원형]의 형태로 바꾸세요.

| do | buy | go |

② 주어진 상황을 설명하세요.

1. He turned off the TV _____ _____ to bed.
   끄다

2. She went to a bookstore _____ _____ a novel.
   소설

3. They need a computer _____ _____ their homework.

B 문법적으로 올바르게 사용된 것을 고르세요.

1. I exercise (in order to lose / in order to losing) weight.
   운동하다

2. I bought a dictionary (to learned / to learn) English.

3. They left early not (to be late / to are late).
   떠났다

4. Henry used a telescope (to examines / to examine) stars.
   망원경

5. John reviewed the notes not (to forgot / to forget) the important points.
   재검토했다   요점(들)

41

Unit 06 in order to / to

C 밑줄 친 부분에 들어갈 말을 만들어서 대화를 완성하세요.

> 보기
> A: Why do you need a computer? (get information / to)
> B: I need it <u>to get information</u>.

필요하다

섭취하다

1. A: Why do you take vitamin C? (stay healthy / in order to)
   B: We take it _____ _____ _____ _____ _____.

2. A: Why did Maria go to the store? (buy some juice / to)
   B: She went there _____ _____ _____ _____.

고대의

3. A: Why did Andy go to Egypt? (see the ancient pyramids / to)
   B: He went to Egypt _____ _____ _____ _____ _____.

택시를 타다 도착하다

4. A: Why is Tammy taking a taxi? (arrive on time / to)
   B: She is taking a taxi _____ _____ _____ _____.

D in order to의 부정형을 사용해서 자연스러운 내용이 되도록 고치세요.

너무 오래 익히다

> 보기
> I turned the oven off in order to overcook the soup.
> → I turned the oven off <u>in order not to overcook</u> the soup.

적어놓았다

1. She wrote down his address <u>to forget</u> it.
   → She wrote down his address _____ it.

놓치다

2. I got up early <u>to miss</u> the bus.
   → I got up early _____ the bus.

돼지 저금통

3. They bought a piggy bank <u>in order to waste</u> money.
   → They bought a piggy bank _____ money.

감기 걸리다

4. We wear sweaters <u>in order to catch</u> a cold.
   → We wear sweaters _____ a cold.

E 보기와 같이 두 문장을 하나로 연결하세요.

> 보기 I went to the park. I wanted to take a walk.
> → I went to the park to take a walk.

1 I call him. I want to say hello. *(전화하다)*

   → _____

2 She will study harder. She wants to pass the exam. *(더 열심히 / 통과하다)*

   → _____

3 He raised his hand. He wanted to ask a question. *(들었다)*

   → _____

4 They went to bed early. They wanted to wake up early in the morning. *(잠자리에 들었다 / 일어나다)*

   → _____

F 주어진 단어들을 바르게 배열하여 문장을 완성하세요. (참고: 영어는 항상 '주어'를 먼저 찾아야 해요.)

1 the window / I / to get fresh air / opened

   → _____

   (나는 상쾌한 공기를 쐬기 위해 창문을 열었다.)

2 to laugh / not / Linda / tried hard *(웃다)*

   → _____

   (Linda는 웃지 않기 위해서 열심히 노력했다.)

3 practiced a lot / in order to / We / win the contest *(연습했다 / 이기다)*

   → _____

   (우리는 대회에서 이기기 위해 많이 연습했다.)

4 to break the glass / walked carefully / not / I *(깨다 / 조심스럽게)*

   → _____

   (나는 유리컵을 깨지 않기 위해서 조심스럽게 걸었다.)

Unit 06 in order to / to

Part 3 Writing Practice

A 주어진 단어들을 활용하여 문장을 영작하세요.

always 항상	America 미국	bring 가져오다	cafeteria 구내식당	check 확인하다
classroom 교실	clean 청소하다	curtain 커튼	enough 충분한	get 받다
help 돕다	lunch 점심	mop 대걸레	need 필요하다	sunlight 햇빛
take out ~을 내놓다	trash 쓰레기	watch 시계	wear (시계를) 차다	

1 나는 교실을 청소하기 위해서 대걸레를 가져왔다.

→ _____

(나는 / 가져왔다 / 대걸레를 / 청소하기 위해서 / 교실을)

2 Jessie는 충분한 햇빛을 받기 위해 커튼을 열었다.

→ _____

(Jessie는 / 열었다 / 커튼을 / 받기 위해 / 충분한 햇빛을)

3 Michelle은 점심을 먹기 위해 구내식당으로 갔다.

→ _____

(Michelle은 / 갔다 / 구내식당으로 / 먹기 위해 / 점심을)

4 그녀는 시간을 확인하기 위해서 항상 시계를 찬다.

→ _____

(그녀는 / 항상 / 시계를 찬다 / 확인하기 위해서 / 시간을)

5 나는 나의 엄마를 돕기 위해 쓰레기를 내놓았다.

→ _____

(나는 / 내놓았다 / 쓰레기를 / 돕기 위해 / 나의 엄마를)

6 미국에 가려면 무엇이 필요합니까?

→ _____

(무엇이 / 내가 / 필요합니까 / 가기 위해 / 미국에)

MUST-HAVE 2

B 주어진 단어들을 활용하여 단락을 완성하세요.

| bike 자전거 | bookstore 서점 | fashion 패션 | magazine 잡지 |
| ride 타다 | stay healthy 건강을 유지하다 | study 연구하다 | trend 동향 |

1 My aunt is studying art to be a fashion designer. _____
(그녀는 / 간다 / 서점에 /

_____. _____
사기 위해 / 패션 잡지들을) (그녀는 / 필요하다 / 그것들이 /

_____. Someday, she will be a famous designer.
연구하기 위해 / 패션 동향을) 유명한

2 My family likes riding bikes. _____.
타는 것 (나의 아빠는 / 자전거를 탄다 / 건강을 유지하기 위해)

_____. And I ride my bike to enjoy myself.
(나의 오빠는 / 자전거를 탄다 / 학교에 가기 위해) 타다 즐기다

C 그림을 묘사해 보세요.

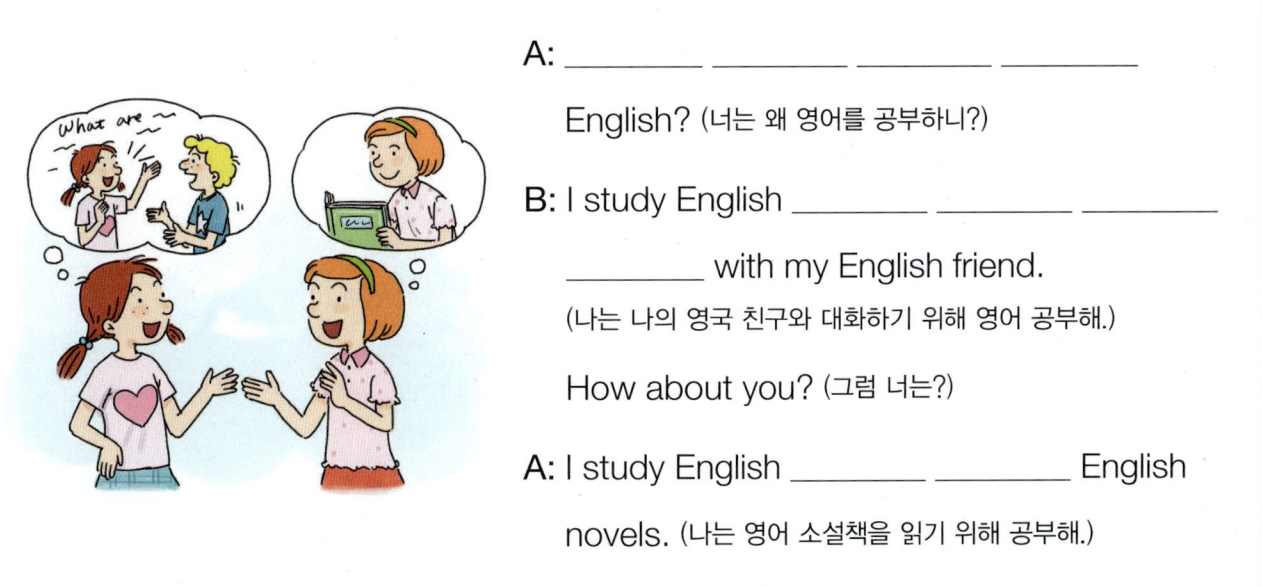

A: ____ ____ ____ ____ English? (너는 왜 영어를 공부하니?)

B: I study English ____ ____ ____ ____ with my English friend.
(나는 나의 영국 친구와 대화하기 위해 영어 공부해.)
How about you? (그럼 너는?)

A: I study English ____ ____ English novels. (나는 영어 소설책을 읽기 위해 공부해.)

* 주요 어휘는 Word Test p.114에서 한 번 더 연습하세요.

Review 02 Play Script

A 아래 그림과 단어박스를 참고하여 대본에 들어갈 내용을 정리하세요.

[Pic 1]   [Pic 2]   [Pic 3]

OUTLINE

Title: *The Ant and the Grasshopper*
개미   메뚜기

Author: Aesop

Characters: ant, grasshopper

Setting: in front of the ant's house
~앞에

Plot: [Pic 1] - The ant asked, "_____ is it?" It was the grasshopper.

- The grasshopper asked for some food.

[Pic 2] - The ant worked hard _____ _____ _____ store food last
          열심히   지난

summer.

- The ant asked, "_____ did you do at that time?"

- The ant asked, "_____ didn't you store any food?"
                                          저장하다

- The grasshopper answered, "I didn't have time."
                  대답했다

[Pic 3] - The grasshopper was so sad and said, "_____ shall I go?"
                            매우   ~해야 한다

in order to	who	why	where	what
~하기 위하여	누구	왜	어디로	무엇을

MUST-HAVE 2

B 아웃라인을 바탕으로 "*The Ant and the Grasshopper*"의 연극 대본을 완성하세요.

The Ant and the Grasshopper

(Knock, knock, knock!)

Ant: _____?

Grasshopper: It's me. I'm hungry. Please give _____ something to eat.
　　　　　　　　　　　　　　　　　　　　　　　무언가　　먹다

Ant: Hmm, I worked hard _____ last summer.
　　　　　　　　　　　　　　　　　　　　　　　　　　　　　　　　　여름

_____ at that time?

Grasshopper: I sang and danced all day long.
　　　　　　　노래했다

Ant: _____?

Grasshopper: I didn't have time. I was very busy singing and dancing.
　　　　　　　　　　　　　　　　　　　　　　　　　　바쁜

Ant: You don't deserve it. I can't give you my food. It is all _____.
　　　～할 자격이 있다　　　　　　　　　　　　　　　　　　　　　　　　닫다
(The ant shuts the door.)

Grasshopper: Oh, my! _____?

✏️ 아래 내용을 모두 잘 학습하였으면 □안에 ✔하세요.

☐ 인칭대명사(I, You, He, She, It)를 맞게 사용하였다.

☐ 의문사(Who, Why, What, Where)를 사용해 의문문을 만들었다.

☐ [in order to/to]를 사용하여 '~하기 위하여'를 표현하였다.

Unit 07 too ~ to / enough to

Part 1 Grammar Point

A [too + 형용사/부사 + to + 동사원형]은 부정의 의미로 '너무 ~해서 … 할 수 없는' 또는 '~ 하기에는 너무 ~ 한' 으로 해석하면 됩니다.

- The problem is too difficult. I can't solve it. 그 문제는 너무 어렵다. 나는 풀 수 없다.
  → The problem is **too** difficult **to** solve. 그 문제는 너무 어려워서 풀 수 없다.
- The food was too hot. I couldn't eat it. 그 음식은 너무 뜨거웠다. 나는 먹을 수가 없었다.
  → The food was **too** hot **to** eat. 그 음식은 너무 뜨거워서 먹을 수가 없었다.

B [too + 형용사/부사 + to + 동사원형]은 [so + 형용사/부사 + that + 주어 + can't(couldn't) + 동사원형]으로 바꿔서 사용할 수 있습니다.

- The box is **too** heavy **to** move. 그 상자는 너무 무거워서 옮길 수 없다.
  = The box is **so** heavy **that I can't** move it.
- The river was **too** wide **to** cross. 그 강은 너무 폭이 넓어서 건널 수 없었다.
  = The river was **so** wide **that** we **couldn't** cross it.

C  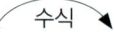 [형용사/부사 + enough to + 동사원형]은 '~할 만큼 충분히 …한', [enough + 명사 + to + 동사원형]은 '~할 만큼 충분한 …' 으로 쓰입니다.

형태	의미
형용사/부사 + enough to + 동사원형	~할 만큼 충분히 …한
enough + 명사 + to + 동사원형	~할 만큼 충분한 …

- Zack is rich **enough to** buy a large apartment. Zack은 큰 아파트를 살 만큼 충분히 부자이다.
- She is strong **enough to** carry the luggage. 그녀는 여행가방을 들 정도로 충분히 힘이 세다.
- I have **enough** money **to** buy a car. 나는 차를 살 충분한 돈이 있다.
- We have **enough** time **to** study for the final exam. 우리는 기말고사를 위해 공부할 충분한 시간이 있다.

Part 2 Grammar Exercise

A 주어진 상황을 설명하기 위해서 [too~to] 또는 [enough to] 구문을 넣어 문장을 완성하세요.

long	tired	study	lift	wear
긴	피곤한	공부하다	들어올리다	입다

1 This skirt is _____ _____ _____ _____.

2 I am _____ _____ _____ _____.

3 Gary is strong _____ _____ _____ the stone.
힘 센   돌/바위

B 밑줄 친 부분이 전달하고자 하는 의미를 살려서 해석하세요.

1 He is <u>too young to understand</u> the book.
   너무 어린

   → 그는 _____.

2 The water <u>is too dirty to drink</u>.
   더러운

   → 그 물은 _____.

3 Jim <u>is tall enough to reach the top shelf</u>.
   키 큰   닿다/도달하다   선반

   → Jim은 _____.

Unit 07 too ~ to / enough to

C 주어진 단어를 알맞은 곳에 넣어 내용을 확장해 보세요.

1 The bag is heavy to carry. (too)
　무거운　휴대하다
→ _____

2 This coat is big to wear. (enough)
　　　입다
→ _____

3 The weather is cold to go for a jog. (too)
→ _____

4 The hero was brave to save the girl. (enough)
　　　용감한　　구하다
→ _____

5 Do you have time to finish the test? (enough)
→ _____

D 두 문장이 같은 뜻이 되도록 문장을 완성하세요.

> 보기 The soup is too salty to eat.
> → The soup is <u>so salty that I can't</u> eat it.
> 　　　　　　　　짠

1 This book is too boring to read.
　　　　　　지루한
→ This book is _____ read it.

2 The tree is too tall to climb.
　　　　　　　오르다
→ The tree is _____ climb it.

3 The dress was too dirty to wear.
→ The dress was _____ wear it.

4 I was too sleepy to do my homework.
　　　　졸린
→ I was _____ do my homework.

E 보기와 같이 두 문장을 한 문장으로 만드세요.

> 보기 This shirt is too small. I can't wear it.
> → This shirt is too small to wear.

보고서/작문/산문   어려운
1 This paper is too difficult. I can't use it.
→ _____

비싼
2 The camera was too expensive. I couldn't buy it.
→ _____

3 The pot is too hot. I can't touch it.
→ _____

잡다/따라잡다
4 The cheetah runs too fast. I can't catch it.
→ _____

F 주어진 단어들을 바르게 배열하여 문장을 완성하세요.(참고:영어는 항상 '주어'를 먼저 찾아야 해요.)

1 is / She / to go to school / too young
→ _____
(그녀는 너무 어려서 학교에 다닐 수 없다.)

외출하다
2 couldn't go out / It was / that I / so cold
→ _____
(날씨가 너무 추워서 나는 외출할 수 없었다.)

부끄러움을 타는
3 to talk to her / was / He / too shy
→ _____
(그는 너무 수줍어서 그녀에게 말을 걸 수 없었다.)

4 studied hard / They / to pass the test / enough
→ _____
(그들은 시험에 통과할 만큼 충분히 열심히 공부했다.)

Unit 07 too ~ to / enough to

Part 3 Writing Practice

A 주어진 단어들을 활용하여 문장을 영작하세요.

bitter 쓴	far away 멀리 떨어진	go on a picnic 소풍을 가다	kind 친절한
medicine 약	nervous 긴장한	painting 그림	people 사람들
poor 가난한	simple 간단한	sleep 자다	take (약을) 먹다
understand 이해하다	visit 방문하다	warm 따뜻한	weather 날씨

1 Dan은 가난한 사람들을 도울 만큼 충분히 친절하다.
   → _____
   (Dan은 / 친절하다 / 충분히 / 도울 만큼 / 가난한 사람들을)

2 Tom은 너무 긴장해서 잠을 잘 수 없었다. (too ~ to)
   → _____
   (Tom은 / 없었다 / 너무 긴장해서 / 잠을 잘 수)

3 날씨가 소풍을 가기에 충분히 따뜻했다.
   → _____
   (날씨가 / 따뜻했다 / 충분히 / 소풍을 가기에)

4 그 약은 너무 써서 먹을 수 없다. (too ~ to)
   → _____
   (그 약은 / 없다 / 너무 써서 / 먹을 수)

5 태양은 너무 멀리 떨어져 있어서 우리가 방문할 수 없다. (so ~ that … can't)
   → _____
   (태양은 / 너무 멀리 떨어져 있어서 / 우리가 / 방문할 수 없다 / 그것을)

6 이 그림은 이해할 수 있을 정도로 충분히 단순하다.
   → _____
   (이 그림은 / 단순하다 / 충분히 / 이해할 수 있을 정도로)

52

MUST-HAVE 2

B 주어진 단어들을 활용하여 단락을 완성하세요.

| animal 동물 | exciting 흥미진진한 | feed 먹이를 주다 | handle 다루다 | heavy 무거운 |
| mirror 거울 | move 옮기다 | some 일부의 | wild 사나운 | zoo 동물원 |

1 I'm packing up for my move. _____.
   짐을 싸다   이사   (이 상자들은 / 없다 / 너무 무거워서 / 다룰 수)

   _____.
   (그 거울은 / 너무 커서 / 나는 / 옮길 수 없다 / 그것을)

   So I need to call the movers to carry them.
                        물건을 옮기는 사람들

2 _____. There are many kinds of
   (그 동물원은 / 흥미진진하다 / 충분히 / 방문하기에)   많은   종류의

   animals to see. _____. But others
                   (일부 동물들은 / 없다 / 너무 사나워서 / 먹이를 줄 수)

   are mild enough to feed.
        온순한   먹이를 주다

C 그림을 묘사해 보세요.

얻었다/받았다   이름이 ~인
We got a new classmate named Sarah.
(우리 반에 Sarah라는 새 친구가 들어왔다.)

I was _____ _____ _____ _____

hello to her.
(나는 너무 수줍어서 그녀에게 인사할 수 없었다.)

But she was _____ _____ _____

_____ to me first.
(하지만 그녀는 나에게 먼저 말을 할 만큼 충분히 친절했다.)

* 주요 어휘는 Word Test p.115에서 한 번 더 연습하세요.

Unit 08 to부정사를 형용사처럼 쓰기

Part 1 Grammar Point

A [to + 동사원형]을 to부정사라고 하며, 문장에서 ①명사, ②형용사, 또는 ③부사의 역할을 합니다.

형 태	to + 동사원형 (긍정) not to + 동사원형 (부정)
쓰 임	①명사적 용법 – 주어, 목적어, 보어 역할 ②형용사적 용법 – 명사를 수식하는 역할 ③부사적 용법 – 목적, 원인, 이유 등과 같은 의미를 나타내는 역할

- I hope **to see** you again. 나는 너를 다시 보기를 바란다. (명사적 용법)
  주어 동사 목적어

- I need some water **to drink**. 나는 마실 물이 필요하다. (형용사적 용법)
  주어 동사 목적어 형용사

- Mark went to the restaurant **to meet** his friends. Mark는 그의 친구들을 만나기 위해 식당에 갔다. (부사적 용법)
  주어 동사 전치사구 부사(동사 수식)

B to부정사가 형용사처럼 쓰일 경우 '~하는 / ~할'이라는 의미로 쓰입니다.

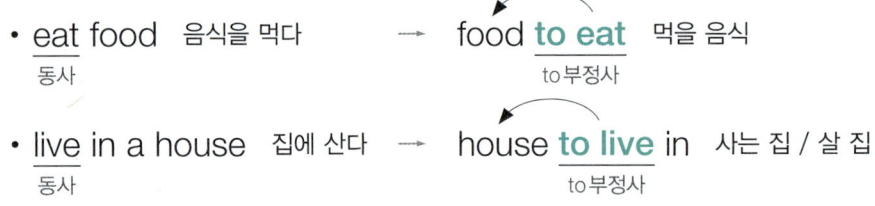

- eat food 음식을 먹다 → food **to eat** 먹을 음식
  동사   to부정사

- live in a house 집에 산다 → house **to live** in 사는 집 / 살 집
  동사   to부정사

C to부정사가 형용사처럼 쓰일 때는 바로 앞에 나오는 명사나 대명사를 수식합니다.

- I have a lot of homework **to do**. 나는 해야 할 숙제가 많이 있다.

- There weren't any movies **to watch**. 볼 영화가 전혀 없었다.

- Do you have something **to tell** me? 당신은 내게 할 말이 있습니까?

Part 2 Grammar Exercise

A ① 주어진 상황을 설명하기 위해서 알맞은 명사와 동사를 선택하세요.

solve	dream	place	be	visit	problem
풀다/해결하다	꿈/꿈꾸다	장소	되다	방문하다	문제

② to부정사를 형용사로 사용해서 내용을 완성하세요.

1  New York has many _____ to _____.

2  My _____ is to _____ a soccer player.

3  Rick has a _____ to _____.

B to부정사의 형용사적 용법으로 사용할 수 있는 것을 고르세요.

1 She needs a dress (to wear / to wore).

2 He wants (to travels / to travel) around the world.
　　　　　　　　　　　　　　　　　　　전 세계 여기 저기

3 We need chairs (to sit / to sat) in.

4 I have a question (to ask / to asked) you.
　　　　　　질문

5 Can you lend me a pen (to using / to use)?
　　　빌려주다

Unit 08 to부정사를 형용사처럼 쓰기

C 밑줄 친 to부정사가 수식하는 말을 찾아 표시하세요.

> 보기
> 나누다/공유하다
> I have a story to share with you.

1 There are many poor people to help.
   가난한

2 They have some furniture to move.
   가구

3 She has a book to return to the library.

4 The students have a report to write.

5 There are some vegetables to buy.

D 각 문장의 내용을 살펴보고, 밑줄 친 부분을 올바르게 해석하세요.

> 보기
> We decided on a place to meet. (만날 장소)
> 결심했다   장소

1 My sister needs more time to prepare for the test. (   )
   준비하다

2 You have many children to take care of. (   )

3 I got some flower seeds to plant. (   )
   씨앗들   심다

4 Here is some food to eat. (   )

5 I know a good place to play badminton. (   )

MUST-HAVE 2

E need가 들어간 문장을 쓰면서, to부정사의 형용사적 용법을 사용하세요.

> 보기
> I don't have a comic book. (read)
> 　　　만화　　책
> → I need a comic book to read.

1 He doesn't have a phone. (call)
→ _____

2 They don't have a table. (put in the kitchen)
　　　　　　　　　　　　　놓다
→ _____

3 She doesn't have a sweater. (wear)
→ _____

4 We don't have friends. (spend time together with)
→ _____

F 주어진 단어들을 바르게 배열하여 문장을 완성하세요.(참고: 영어는 항상 '주어*'를 먼저 찾아야 해요.)

1 have / I* / to memorize / some words
　　　　　　　외우다
→ _____
(나는 외워야 할 단어가 몇 개 있다.)

2 some friends / has / Jean* / to visit
　　　　　　　　　　　　　방문하다
→ _____
(Jean은 방문할 몇 명의 친구가 있다.)

3 to set / had / several tables / They*
　　　　　　　여러 개/몇몇
→ _____
(그들은 차려야 할 테이블이 여러 개 있었다.)

4 to ride / needs a bike / Peter* / to school
→ _____
(Peter는 학교에 타고 갈 자전거가 필요하다.)

57

Unit 08 to부정사를 형용사처럼 쓰기

Part 3 Writing Practice

A 주어진 단어들을 활용하여 문장을 영작하세요.

adult 어른	best 최적의	children 아이들	costume 의상	England 영국
find 발견하다	help 돕다	interesting 재미있는	many 많은	money 돈
need 필요하다	novel 소설	on Halloween 할로윈에	spend (돈, 시간)을 쓰다	thing 일
this 이것, 지금	today 오늘	wear 입다		

1 나는 읽을 만한 재미있는 소설을 발견했다.

→ _____

(나는 / 발견했다 / 재미있는 / 소설을 / 읽을 만한)

2 너는 할로윈에 입을 의상을 샀니?

→ _____

(너는 / 샀니 / 의상을 / 입을 / 할로윈에)

3 나는 오늘 해야 할 많은 일이 있다.

→ _____

(나는 / (가지고) 있다 / 많은 일이 / 해야 할 / 오늘)

4 지금이 영국을 방문할 최적의 시기이다.

→ _____

(지금 / 이다 / 최적의 시간 / 방문할 / 영국을)

5 그녀는 쓸 돈을 가지고 있지 않았다.

→ _____

(그녀는 / 가지고 있지 않았다 / 돈을 / 쓸)

6 그 아이들은 도와줄 어른이 필요하다.

→ _____

(그 아이들은 / 필요하다 / 어른이 / 도와줄)

MUST-HAVE 2

B 주어진 단어들을 활용하여 단락을 완성하세요.

| advice 조언 | always 항상 | computer 컴퓨터 | fix 고치다 | give 주다 |
| homework 숙제 | repairman 수리공 | someone 누군가 | talk 이야기하다 | want 원하다 |

1 _____. She decides to talk to
  (Julie는 / 원한다 / 누군가를 / 이야기할)   결심하다

her teacher. _____
              (그녀의 선생님은 / 항상 / 가지고 있다 / 좋은 조언을 /

_____.
줄 (수 있는))

2 _____ on the computer. But he couldn't
  (그는 / 가지고 있었다 / 숙제를 / 해야 할)

do it because his computer was broken. So _____
       ~때문에   고장난   (그의 아빠는 / 전화했다 /

_____.
수리공에게 / 고쳐줄 / 그것을)

C 그림을 묘사해 보세요.

        ~이 있다   방법들
There are some ways _____ _____

_____. (건강을 유지하는 몇 가지 방법이 있다.)
가지다/취하다
Take 30 minutes _____ _____

_____. (운동할 30분을 내라.)
시도하다
Try _____ _____ _____ too
        많은
much food at one time.
(한 번에 너무 많은 음식을 먹지 않도록 해라.)

* 주요 어휘는 Word Test p.115에서 한 번 더 연습하세요.

Unit 09 to부정사를 부사처럼 쓰기

Part 1 Grammar Point

A to부정사는 부사처럼 앞에 나온 형용사를 수식합니다.

- The glass is easy <u>to break</u>. 그 유리는 깨지기 쉽다.
- The icy road is dangerous <u>to drive</u> on. 그 빙판길은 운전하기 위험하다.
- He is likely <u>to come</u> home soon. 그는 곧 집에 올 것 같다.

B 매일 사용하는 감정 형용사 10개가 있어요. 이 형용사들을 꾸며주기 위해서 그 뒤에 to부정사를 쓸 수 있어요.

be동사 + 감정 형용사 + to부정사	의미	예문
be afraid to	~하기가 두렵다	He was afraid to tell her the secret. 그는 그녀에게 비밀을 말하기가 두려웠다.
be careful to	~하기 조심스럽다	She was careful to touch the big dog. 그녀는 그 큰 개를 만지기 조심스러웠다.
be disappointed to	~해서 실망하다	We were disappointed to fail the test. 우리는 시험에 떨어져서 실망했다.
be glad/happy to	~해서 기쁘다	I am happy to meet you. 너를 만나서 기쁘다.
be lucky to	운 좋게 ~하다	He was lucky to take the last train. 그는 운 좋게 마지막 기차를 탔다.
be proud to	~해서 자랑스럽다	I am proud to be a part of your team. 나는 당신 팀의 일원이 되어 자랑스럽다.
be sad to	~해서 슬프다	We were sad to see him leave. 우리는 그가 떠나는 것을 보고 슬펐다.
be sorry to	~해서 유감이다	I am sorry to hear the bad news. 안 좋은 소식을 듣게 되어 유감이다.
be surprised to	~해서 놀라다	She is surprised to find out the truth. 그녀는 진실을 알고 놀랐다.

MUST-HAVE 2

Part 2 Grammar Exercise

A ① 주어진 상황과 어울리는 형용사와 동사를 고르세요.

hear	happy	meet	proud	surprised	win
듣다	행복한	만나다	자랑스러운	놀란	이기다

② 형용사 뒤에 to부정사를 써서 내용을 완성하세요.

1 The girl was _____ to _____ the news.

2 We are _____ to _____ the game.

3 I am _____ to _____ my old friend.

　　　　　　　　　　　　　　　　　　　　　　　　　　　옛날

B '형용사 + to부정사'의 역할을 살려서 밑줄 친 부분을 해석하세요.

　　　　　　어려운
1 The paper <u>is difficult to understand</u>.

　→ 그 논문은 _____.

　　　　　　준비된
2 They <u>are ready to start</u> the race.

　→ 그들은 경기를 _____.

　　　　　　　　　　　　믿다
3 The story <u>was hard to believe</u>.

　→ 그 이야기는 _____.

　　　　　　　　　쉬운　　　대답하다
4 The question <u>is not easy to answer</u>.

　→ 그 질문은 _____.

61

Unit 09 to부정사를 부사처럼 쓰기

C 내용의 완성을 위해서 가장 어울리는 표현을 골라 문장을 완성하세요.

| be surprised to 놀라다 | be disappointed to 실망하다 | be likely to |
| be sorry to 미안하다/유감이다 | be glad to 기쁘다 | |

1 Hi, Jamie. I _____ see you again.
　　　　　　　　　　　　　　　　다시

2 I _____ wake you up so early.

3 A concert ticket _____ be expensive.

4 He _____ get the low scores on the test yesterday.

5 They _____ see a ghost last night.

D 밑줄 친 부분을 올바르게 배열해 보세요.

| 보기 | Tony was to visit happy his grandparents again. |
| | 　　　　(①)　　(③)　　(②)　　　　할아버지와 할머니 |

1 Sam to eat was afraid the spicy food.
　　　　(　)　(　)　(　)　　두려운　매운

2 I lucky am to have so many friends.
　　운이 좋은
　　(　)　(　)　(　)

3 She to be proud is on the national team.
　　　　(　)　　(　)　(　)　자랑스러운　　국가의

4 He was to lose sad his dog.
　　(　)　(　)　(　)

5 I ready was to win the singing contest.
　　(　)　(　)　(　)

E 주어진 to부정사를 알맞은 곳에 넣어 문장을 완성하세요.

　　　　　　　　　기쁜
1 Dan was glad the old people. (to help)

→ _____

　　　　　　　　　　간절히 바라는
2 Many people are eager English. (to learn)

→ _____

　　　　　　　　　　　　낯선 사람들
3 Jane is afraid to strangers. (to talk)

→ _____

　　　　　　살아있는　　　　　　지진
4 We are lucky alive after the earthquake. (to be)

→ _____

　　　　　　　　　　　　떠나다
5 Ben was sad his family. (to leave)

→ _____

F 주어진 단어들을 바르게 배열하여 문장을 완성하세요.(참고: 영어는 항상 주어를 먼저 찾아야* 해요.)

1 to break / Bad habits* / easy / are not
　　　　　　　습관들

→ _____

(나쁜 습관은 깨기 쉽지 않다.)

2 to buy / I am* / happy / the book

→ _____

(나는 그 책을 사게 되어 기쁘다.)

3 is / to walk on / dangerous / The wet floor*
　　　　　　　　　　위험한

→ _____

(젖은 마루는 걷기 위험하다.)

4 very sorry / I am* / to bother / you
　　　　　　　　　　　　방해하다

→ _____

(너를 귀찮게 해서 매우 미안하다.)

Unit 09 to부정사를 부사처럼 쓰기

Part 3 Writing Practice

A 주어진 단어들을 활용하여 문장을 영작하세요.

> at the door 현관에서　broken 깨진　come true 이루어지다　dream 꿈
> hard 어려운　join 가입하다　know 알다　report 보고서
> school band 학교 밴드　see 보다　truth 진실　understand 이해하다
> window 창문

1 너의 보고서는 이해하기 어렵다.

→ _____

(너의 보고서는 / 어렵다 / 이해하기)

2 우리는 그 진실을 알고 실망했다.

→ _____

(우리는 / 실망했다 / 알고 / 그 진실을)

3 나는 학교 밴드에 가입하여 기쁘다.

→ _____

(나는 / 기쁘다 / 가입하여 / 학교 밴드에)

4 그는 깨진 창문을 발견하고 화가 났다.

→ _____

(그는 / 화가 났다 / 발견하고 / 깨진 창문을)

5 Dorothy는 현관에서 그를 보고 놀랐다.

→ _____

(Dorothy는 / 놀랐다 / 보고 / 그를 / 현관에서)

6 그의 꿈은 이루어질 수 있을 것 같다.

→ _____

(그의 꿈은 / 있을 것 같다 / 이루어질 수)

B 주어진 단어들을 활용하여 단락을 완성하세요.

| believe 믿다 | hear 듣다 | in front of ~앞에 | member 회원 |
| news 소식 | people 사람들 | speak 말하다 | speech club 웅변클럽 |

1 _____. At first,
   (나는 / 자랑스럽다 / 회원인 것이 / 웅변클럽의)   첫 번째로

I had a small and low voice. Moreover, _____
                 게다가/더욱이   (나는 / 두려웠다 / 말하는 것이 /

_____. But thanks to the club, I have no fear of giving speeches.
앞에서 / 많은 사람들)   고맙다   공포/무서움   연설

2 Andy won a scholarship from the school. _____
      장학금을 탔다   (그는 / 놀랐다 /

_____. _____.
듣고 / 그 소식을)   (그 소식은 / 어려웠다 / 믿기)

Now he is likely to study even harder.
         ~ 할 것 같은   심지어

C 그림을 묘사해 보세요.

At first, Sally _____ _____ _____ leave   (떠나다)

her friends. (처음에 Sally는 친구들을 떠나게 되어 슬펐다.)

Now, however, she _____ _____ _____

_____ her new friends.

(그러나 지금 그녀는 새로운 친구들을 만나 행복하다.)

She _____ _____ _____ _____ a

good time with them.

(그녀는 그들과 좋은 시간을 보낼 수 있을 것 같다.)

* 주요 어휘는 Word Test p.116에서 한 번 더 연습하세요.

Review 03 Essay

A 아래 표를 참고하여 내가 필요한 세 가지에 대한 글에 들어갈 내용을 정리하세요.

	Needs 필요한 것	Features 특징들
Person	a friend to talk with	friendly enough to listen to what I am saying 친절한
Animal	a pet to play with 애완동물	lovely enough to relieve my stress 사랑스러운　　줄이다
Object	a computer to help me with my homework	powerful enough to solve any difficult problems 강한

OUTLINE

Title What I Need Most
　　　　　　　　가장

Beginning three things that I need most

Middle　Person: - a friend _____ _____ with; friendly enough to listen to what I am saying

　　　　　Animal: - a pet _____ _____ with; lovely _____ _____ relieve my stress

　　　　　Object: - my mom is too busy to help me
　　　　　　　　 - a computer _____ _____ me with my homework; powerful _____ _____ solve any difficult problems
　　　　　　　　　　　　　　　　　　　　　　　　　　　　　　　어떤　어려운

Ending I will be happy to have them all.
　　　　　　　　　　　　　　　가지다

---

relieve (불쾌감)을 없애다　　　solve 해결하다　　　stress 스트레스

B 아웃라인을 바탕으로 내가 필요한 것들에 대한 에세이를 완성하세요.

What I Need Most — Title

There are _____. — Beginning

First, I need _____. I hope she(he) is

_____ what I am saying.

Second, I _____. I hope it is

_____.

Third, I have lots of homework. My mom is often _____
많은
_____ me. So I need a computer _____

_____. I hope it is _____. — Middle

I will _____ all. — Ending

아래 내용을 모두 잘 학습하였으면 □안에 ✔하세요.

☐ [too~to]와 [enough to]의 구문을 맞게 사용하였다.

☐ to부정사를 형용사처럼 맞게 사용하였다.

☐ to부정사를 부사처럼 맞게 사용하였다.

Unit 10. to부정사·동명사를 목적어로 쓰기

Part 1 Grammar Point

A 동사의 목적어로써 명사를 쓸 수 있어요. 이 명사(목적어) 자리에 to부정사도 쓸 수 있습니다. 여기 나와 있는 동사들은 그 뒤에 to부정사 쓰는 것을 좋아합니다.

타동사 + to부정사	예 문
agree, ask, choose, decide, forget, hope, learn, need, plan, promise, try, want 등 + to do	• I agreed to go with him. 나는 그와 함께 가는 것에 동의했다. • I decided not to waste my time. 나는 나의 시간을 낭비하지 않기로 결정했다. • We hope to have a safe trip. 우리는 안전한 여행을 하기를 희망한다. • I planned to go shopping today. 나는 오늘 쇼핑 갈 것을 계획하였다. • We tried to finish it on time. 우리는 제시간에 그것을 끝내려고 노력했다. • I want to take a break. 나는 휴식을 취하길 원한다.

* to부정사를 목적어로 취하는 동사는 Appendix p.110 참고

B 특정 타동사들은 to부정사가 아닌 동명사를 목적어로 쓰는 것을 선호합니다.

타동사 + 동명사	예 문
avoid, enjoy, finish, give up, mind, quit 등 + doing	• Nancy enjoys singing. Nancy는 노래하는 것을 즐긴다. • My sister finished baking bread. 나의 여동생은 빵 굽는 것을 끝냈다. • I gave up losing weight. 나는 체중을 줄이는 것을 포기했다. • My father quit drinking last week. 나의 아버지는 지난주에 술을 끊었다.

* 동명사를 목적어로 취하는 동사 모음은 Appendix p.110 참고

Part 2 Grammar Exercise

A ① 주어진 상황을 설명하기 위해서 가장 적절한 동사를 고르세요.

buy	decide	get up	go	plan	want
사다	결심하다	일어나다	가다	계획하다	원하다

② 상황에 맞도록 문장을 완성하세요.

1 She _____ to _____ the book yesterday.
어제

2 Jack _____ to _____ to a winter camp.

3 I don't _____ to _____ early in the morning.

B to부정사 또는 동명사 중 문법적으로 올바른 것을 고르세요.

1 She promised (to be / being) there on time.
    약속했다   정시에

2 They agreed (working / to work) with us.
    동의했다

3 Cindy enjoys (to visit / visiting) garage sales.
                                         중고물품   세일

4 We need (finishing / to finish) this book.

5 I didn't mind (sharing / to share) my cookie.
    신경쓰지 않는다/괜찮다

Unit 10 to부정사 · 동명사를 목적어로 쓰기

C 밑줄 친 부분을 올바르게 고쳐서 문장을 완성하세요.

> 보기 Bob promised <u>fixing</u> the radio.
>   약속했다
>   → Bob promised to fix the radio.

1 They plan <u>buying</u> a new car.
   → They plan _____ a new car.

2 I enjoy <u>to write</u> letters to my friends.
   → I enjoy _____ letters to my friends.

3 She didn't agree <u>share</u> her room.
   → She didn't agree _____ her room.

4 I hope <u>moving</u> to the country.
   → I hope _____ to the country.

D to부정사의 올바른 위치를 생각해 보면서 밑줄 친 부분을 바르게 배열하세요.

> 보기   기대하다
>   We expect   you   to see   again   soon.
>   (①)   (③)   (②)

1 Jay <u>to stay</u> <u>chose</u> <u>with us</u>.
        머물다   선택했다
        ( )   ( )   ( )

2 Sam <u>hopes</u> <u>to his hometown</u> <u>to return</u>.
                                              돌아가다
        ( )   ( )   ( )

3 She <u>to teach</u> <u>tried</u> <u>Helen</u> table manners.
                                                     식사   예절
        ( )   ( )   ( )

4 Harry <u>quit</u> <u>computer games</u> <u>playing</u>.
          그만두다
          ( )   ( )   ( )

5 They <u>their plans</u> <u>to change</u> <u>decided</u>.
                              변경하다
         ( )   ( )   ( )

70

MUST-HAVE 2

E 내용과 어울리는 동사를 골라 to부정사 또는 동명사로 바꿔 문장을 완성하세요.

read	send	study	go	close
읽다	보내다	공부하다	가다	닫다

1 Some students chose _____ at the library.
                  선택했다   도서관

2 My father promised _____ me the package.
                                                         소포

3 Would you mind _____ the window for me?
      괜찮을까요?/싫어할까요?

4 Mac's family decided _____ to America.

5 I enjoy _____ books in bed.
                                         침대

F 주어진 단어들을 바르게 배열하여 문장을 완성하세요.(참고:영어는 항상 '주어*'를 먼저 찾아야 해요.)

1 with us / wants* / Becky / to have dinner*(저녁)

   → _____

   (Becky는 우리와 함께 저녁을 먹고 싶어한다.)

2 to become / My sister / decided* / a singer
      ~이 되다

   → _____

   (내 여동생은 가수가 되기로 결심했다.)

3 tried to / work out / Jody* / every day

   → _____

   (Jody는 매일 운동하려고 노력했다.)

4 with his help / I* / writing the report / could finish*(할 수 있었다)

   → _____

   (나는 그의 도움을 받아 보고서 쓰기를 끝낼 수 있었다.)

Unit 10 to부정사 · 동명사를 목적어로 쓰기

Part 3 Writing Practice

A 주어진 단어들을 활용하여 문장을 영작하세요.

call 전화하다	country 나라	everyone 모두	for a while 당분간
invite 초대하다	keep the peace 평화를 유지하다	light 불, 빛	meet 만나다
party 파티	today 오늘	too much 너무 많이	turn off 끄다

1 나는 오늘 너를 만나길 바란다.

→ _____

(나는 / 바란다 / 만나길 / 너를 / 오늘)

2 그는 불을 끄는 것을 잊어버렸다.

→ _____

(그는 / 잊어버렸다 / 끄는 것을 / 불을)

3 Naomi는 그녀의 어머니에게 전화하기로 약속했었다.

→ _____

(Naomi는 / 약속했었다 / 전화하기로 / 그녀의 어머니에게)

4 우리는 파티에 모두 초대하기로 결정했다.

→ _____

(우리는 / 결정했다 / 초대하기로 / 모두 / 파티에)

5 그 두 나라는 평화를 유지하기로 동의했다.

→ _____

(그 두 나라는 / 동의했다 / 평화를 유지하기로)

6 당분간 너무 많이 말하는 것을 피하세요. (Avoid로 시작하는 명령문)

→ _____

(피하다 / 말하는 것을 / 너무 많이 / 당분간)

MUST-HAVE 2

B 주어진 단어들을 활용하여 단락을 완성하세요.

always 항상	concert 콘서트	do volunteer work 자원봉사를 하다	favorite 좋아하는
friend 친구	help 돕다	others 다른 사람들	singer 가수
there 거기서	together 함께		

1 My sister wants to see a movie with me. But I can't go with her. _____
~와 함께 (나는 / 계획했다 /

_____. _____
갈 것을 / 콘서트에 / 나의 친구들과) (나는 / 기대한다 / 볼 것을 /

_____. I will go to the theater with my sister next time.
내가 가장 좋아하는 가수를 / 거기서)   극장   다음

2 My friend Kevin is kind. _____.
친절한   (그는 / 항상 / 즐거워한다 / 도와주는 것을 / 다른 사람들을)

_____.
(Kevin과 나는 / 결정했다 / 자원봉사하기로 / 함께)

We will visit a nursing home tomorrow.
양로원

C 그림을 묘사해 보세요.

I _____ _____ _____ to England this summer. (나는 이번 여름에 영국에 갈 계획이다.)
아마도
Maybe I _____ _____ _____ English.
(나는 아마도 영어 공부를 할 필요가 있다.)
좋은
I _____ _____ _____ a great time.
(나는 좋은 시간을 갖기를 바란다.)

* 주요 어휘는 Word Test p.116에서 한 번 더 연습하세요.

Unit 11 to부정사를 목적격 보어로 쓰기

Part 1 Grammar Point

A 목적어가 무엇을 할지 또는 무엇이 될지 부연 설명해줄 수 있어요. 이때 to부정사를 목적어 뒤에 쓰면 됩니다

> 동사 + 목적어(O) + to부정사: 목적어가 ~ 하기를 / ~ 하는것을 / ~ 가 되기를

- I want **you** / **to join** this club. 　나는 네가 이 동아리에 가입하기를 원한다.
  (보어)
- She expects **him** / **to be** a pianist. 　그녀는 그가 피아니스트가 되기를 기대한다.
  (보어)

B to부정사를 목적격 보어로 쓰는 것을 선호하는 동사들을 외워두세요. 매일 사용하는 단어들입니다.

동사 + 목적어(O) + to부정사	의 미	예 문
tell O to do	~에게 …하라고 말하다	He **told** me **to go** there. 그는 내게 거기에 가라고 말했다.
expect O to do	~에게 …하기를 기대하다	She **expects** him **to come** today. 그녀는 그가 오늘 오기를 기대하고 있다.
force O to do	~에게 …하도록 강요하다	They **forced** me **to do** it. 그들은 내게 그것을 하도록 강요했다.
encourage O to do	~에게 …하도록 격려하다	I **encouraged** him **to study** hard. 나는 그가 공부를 열심히 하도록 격려했다.
ask O to do	~에게 …하도록 부탁하다	He **asked** me **to help** him. 그는 내게 그를 돕도록 부탁했다.
allow O to do	~에게 …하도록 허락하다	She **allowed** me **to go** out. 그녀는 내게 외출하도록 허락했다.
advise O to do	~에게 …하도록 조언하다	We **advised** her **to stay** here. 우리는 그녀에게 여기에 머물도록 조언했다.
order O to do	~에게 …하도록 명령하다	I **ordered** them **to start** at once. 나는 그들에게 즉시 시작하도록 명령했다.
want O to do	~에게 …하기를 원하다	The child **wants** his mom **to buy** him the toy. 그 아이는 엄마가 자신에게 장난감을 사주기를 원한다.

Part 2 Grammar Exercise

A ① 주어진 상황과 가장 잘 어울리는 동사를 고르세요.

expect	encourage	allow	take	come	finish
기대하다	격려하다	허락하다	(사진)찍다	오다	마치다

② 빈칸에 적절한 표현을 써서 내용을 완성하세요.

1. Mom _____ me to _____ my homework every day.

2. We didn't _____ him to _____ back soon.

3. The gallery usually _____ us to _____ pictures.
   미술관   보통   사진들

B to부정사를 목적격 보어로 사용한 것을 고르세요.

1. My teacher encouraged (to read me / me to read) many books.
   격려했다

2. Terry wanted (to help her friend / her friend to help) her.

3. Henry asked (me not to forget / not to forget me) his address.

4. Mom allowed (to go out me / me to go out) after dinner.
   허락했다

5. His sister advised (him to be polite / to be polite him) to the elderly.
   충고해주었다   공손한   어르신들

Unit 11 to부정사를 목적격 보어로 쓰기

C 각 문장의 목적어가 하거나 또는 하지 말아야 하는 일을 해석하세요.

1 My father wants me to water the plants.   (물을 주다 / 식물들)
   → 나의 아버지는 _____ 원한다.

2 We asked them not to make any noise.   (소리/잡음)
   → 우리는 _____ 부탁했다.

3 The school ordered us to wear uniforms.   (명령했다/주문했다)
   → 학교는 _____ 지시했다.

4 The dentist advised her not to eat too many sweets.   (사탕)
   → 그 치과의사는 _____ 충고했다.

5 The teacher ordered me to sit down.
   → 선생님은 _____ 명령했다.

D 밑줄 친 부분을 문법적으로 올바르게 고치세요.

> 보기   My brother asked me help with his homework.
> → My brother asked me to help with his homework.

1 Mom wants me care for my brother.   (돌보다)
   → Mom wants me _____ for my brother.

2 Michael advised me to got along with my classmates.   (사이좋게 지내다)
   → Michael advised me _____ along with my classmates.

3 My teacher allowed Susie leaving early.
   → My teacher allowed Susie _____ early.

4 Jack told me not swimming in the deep sea.   (깊은)
   → Jack told me not _____ in the deep sea.

E 보기와 같이 주어진 두 문장을 한 문장으로 연결하세요.

> 보기 He told me. Don't be late for school.
> → He told me not to be late for school.

1 Frank encouraged us. Don't lose hope.
→ _____

2 They expected him. Don't skip class.
→ _____

3 Vicky wants me. Don't waste time.
→ _____

4 We told them. Don't take the bus.
→ _____

5 I advised her. Don't drink too much soda.
→ _____

F 주어진 단어들을 바르게 배열하여 문장을 완성하세요.(참고: 영어는 항상 '주어'를 먼저 찾아야 해요.)

1 to eat food / never forced / My mom / us
→ _____
(나의 엄마는 우리에게 음식을 먹으라고 강요한 적이 없었다.)

2 don't allow / to stay out late / me / My parents
→ _____
(나의 부모님은 내가 밖에서 늦게까지 있는 것을 허락하지 않는다.)

3 told / Our teacher / to recycle paper bags / us
→ _____
(우리 선생님은 우리에게 종이가방을 재활용하라고 말했다.)

4 to work out regularly / advised / The doctor / me
→ _____
(그 의사는 내게 규칙적으로 운동하라고 조언했다.)

Unit 11 to부정사를 목적격 보어로 쓰기

Part 3 Writing Practice

A 주어진 단어들을 활용하여 문장을 영작하세요.

> bank 은행 become 되다 computer game 컴퓨터 게임
> drink 마시다 milk 우유 people 사람들
> play (게임을) 하다 run a race 경주를 하다 save money 저축하다
> skip meals 식사를 거르다 writer 작가

1 나는 그가 작가가 될 것을 기대하지 않았다.
→ _____
   (나는 / 기대하지 않았다 / 그가 / 될 것을 / 작가가)

2 그녀는 내게 식사를 거르지 말라고 말했다.
→ _____
   (그녀는 / 말했다 / 내게 / 거르지 말라고 / 식사를)

3 은행은 사람들에게 저축하도록 장려한다.
→ _____
   (은행(들)은/ 장려한다 / 사람들에게 / 저축하도록)

4 우리 엄마는 우리가 우유를 마시기를 원한다.
→ _____
   (우리 엄마는 / 원한다 / 우리가 / 마시기를 / 우유를)

5 그녀는 내게 컴퓨터 게임을 하지 말라고 조언했다.
→ _____
   (그녀는 / 조언했다 / 내게 / 하지 않을 것을 / 컴퓨터 게임을)

6 우리는 그가 경주를 하지 않을 것이라고 기대했다.
→ _____
   (우리는/ 기대했다 / 그가 / 하지 않을 것을 / 경주를)

MUST-HAVE 2

B 주어진 단어들을 활용하여 단락을 완성하세요.

ask 묻다	eat 먹다	fat 지방	late 늦게
scientist 과학자	stay up 자지 않고 있다	too much 너무 많은	

1 _____. _____
 (나의 엄마는 / 원했다 / 내가 / 되기를 / 과학자가)   (그녀는 / 격려했다 /

_____ as many questions as possible. She advised me to watch
내게 / 묻기를)   가능한 많은 질문들   조언을 해주다/충고하다

everything around me. That is how I became interested in science.
                                      흥미를 가지게 된   과학

2 Dr. Chen gave me a lot of advice to get healthy. _____
           조언/충고   건강해지다   (그는 / 허락하지 않았다 / 내가 /

_____. _____
자지 않고 있는 것을 / 늦게까지)   (그는 / 조언했다 / 내게 /

_____. I made up my mind to listen to his advice.
먹지 말라고 / 너무 많은 / 지방을)   결심하다/마음을 정하다

C 그림을 묘사해 보세요.

Ms. White _____ _____ _____

_____ the flowers in the vase.
(White 선생님은 우리에게 화병에 있는 꽃을 그리라고 말했다.)

She _____ _____ _____ _____ any

colors. (그녀는 우리가 어떤 색이든 쓰도록 허락했다.)

She _____ _____ _____ _____ be
         그리는 것
afraid of drawing pictures.
(그녀는 우리에게 그림 그리는 것을 두려워하지 말라고 조언했다.)

* 주요 어휘는 Word Test p.117에서 한 번 더 연습하세요.

Unit 12 -thing + 형용사

Part 1 Grammar Point

A 형용사는 주로 명사 앞에 씁니다. 그러나 -thing으로 끝나는 부정대명사는 형용사를 그 뒤에 써줍니다. 이유는 부정대명사(~thing)를 강조하기 위해서입니다.

- There is some**thing** mysterious about him.   그에게는 (무언가) 불가사의한 점이 있다.
- Did I miss any**thing** interesting?   내가 (무언가) 재미있는 것을 놓쳤나요?
- There is no**thing** unusual about her.   그녀에게는 특이한 점이 (아무것도) 없다.

B -thing이 붙는 부정대명사들은 평서문, 의문문, 부정문에서 그 의미가 조금씩 다릅니다.

부정대명사	쓰 임	의 미	예 문
something	평서문	어떤 것, 무언가	There is **something** wrong. 잘못된 (어떤) 것이 있다.
	의문문 (권유, 부탁의 경우)	어떤 것, 무언가	Would you like to eat **something** sweet? 달콤한 (어떤) 것을 드시겠어요?
anything	평서문	무엇이든	I like **anything** exciting. 나는 신나는 것을 (무엇이든) 좋아한다.
	부정문	아무것도	I don't like **anything** boring. 나는 따분한 것을 (아무것도) 좋아하지 않는다.
	의문문	무언가	Is there **anything** good? (무언가) 좋은 것이 있나요?
nothing (= not + anything)	모든 문장 형식	아무것도 없음	There is **nothing** special in this movie. 이 영화에는 특별한 것이 (아무것도) 없다.

Part 2 Grammar Exercise

A 내용상 가장 적절한 부정대명사와 형용사를 골라 주어진 상황을 설명하세요.

nothing	something	anything	dangerous	cold	new
아무것도	뭔가	아무것도	위험한	차가운	새로운

1
I want _____ _____ for my room.

2
She doesn't drink _____ _____.

3
There is _____ _____ here.
~이 있다

B anything, something, nothing의 쓰임이 올바른 것을 고르세요.

1 She doesn't like (sad anything / anything sad).
  슬픈

2 Is there (wrong anything / anything wrong) with the plan?
  잘못된

3 I want to eat (something delicious / delicious something).
  맛있는

4 There is (bad nothing / nothing bad) about it.
  나쁜

5 Can you do (something special / special something) for me?
  특별한

Unit 12 -thing + 형용사

C 밑줄 친 부분을 해석해서 전체 내용을 완성하세요.

1 I want to buy <u>something nice and valuable</u>.
   (가치있는)
   → 나는 _____ 사길 원한다.

2 Jean felt <u>something soft</u> under her feet.
   (느꼈다)   (~아래에)
   → Jane은 발 밑에서 _____ 느꼈다.

3 There is <u>nothing exciting to watch</u> on TV now.
   (신나는)
   → 지금 TV에는 _____.

4 The doctor told me not to eat <u>anything sweet</u>.
   (단/단맛이 나는)
   → 의사는 내게 _____ 먹지 말라고 말했다.

5 Is there <u>anything important</u> in the box?
   (중요한)
   → 그 상자 안에 _____ 있니?

D 내용상 가장 적절하고 자연스러운 부정대명사를 고르세요.

1 I don't expect (anything / something / nothing) perfect.
   (기대하다)   (완벽한)

2 I'm bored. Would you show me (anything / something / nothing) funny?
   (지루한)   (보여주다)   (재미있는)

3 I don't have much money. I won't buy (anything / something / nothing) expensive.
                                                                              (비싼)

4 The food is not special. There is (anything / something / nothing) unique about it.
                                                                        (독특한/고유의)

5 The speech was great. I learned (anything / something / nothing) important.
      (연설)

6 There is (anything / something / nothing) wrong with this computer. It works well.
                                                                                (작동하다)

E 주어진 단어를 알맞은 곳에 넣어 문장을 완성하세요.

1 I'm looking for special. (something)   *찾는 중*
   → _____

2 There is serious to worry about. (nothing)   *심각한*
   → _____

3 Some people should not eat sweet. (anything)
   → _____

4 We found funny in this photo. (something)   *찾았다*
   → _____

5 She doesn't want to hear bad. (anything)
   → _____

F 주어진 단어들을 바르게 배열하여 문장을 완성하세요. (참고: 영어는 항상 '주어'를 먼저 찾아야 해요.)

1 to buy / different / Pam wants / something   *다른*
   → _____
   (Pam은 다른 (어떤) 것을 사길 원한다.)

2 in this picture / anything / I don't see / strange   *이상한*
   → _____
   (나는 이 그림에서 이상한 것은 아무것도 보이지 않는다.)

3 in that game / There was / fun / nothing
   → _____
   (그 게임에는 재미있는 것이 아무것도 없었다.)

4 anything / loves to have / The little girl / pink
   → _____
   (그 어린 소녀는 핑크색인 것은 무엇이든 갖고 싶어한다.)

Unit 12 -thing + 형용사

Part 3 Writing Practice

A 주어진 단어들을 활용하여 문장을 영작하세요.

creative 창의적인	during the game 경기 중에	happen to ~에게 일어나다	important 중요한
invention 발명품	magic 마술	new 새로운	old man 노인
strange 이상한	teach 가르치다	teacher 선생님	want 원하다
wonderful 놀라운	wrong 잘못된		

1 그의 마술에는 놀라운 (어떤) 것이 있다.

→ _____

(있다 / (어떤) 것이 / 놀라운 / 그의 마술에는)

2 나는 경기 중에 잘못된 것은 하지 않았다. (anything)

→ _____

(나는* / 하지 않았다 / 것은 / 잘못된 / 경기 중에)

3 그의 발명품에는 새로운 것이 아무것도 없었다. (nothing)

→ _____

(아무것도 없었다 / 새로운 것이 / 그의 발명품에는)

4 나의 선생님은 나에게서 창의적인 (어떤) 것을 원한다.

→ _____

(나의 선생님은* / 원한다 / (어떤) 것을 / 창의적인 / 나에게서)

5 그 노인은 우리에게 중요한 (어떤) 것을 가르쳤다.

→ _____

(그 노인은* / 가르쳤다 / 우리에게 / (어떤) 것을 / 중요한)

6 어떤 이상한 일이 그에게 일어났다.

→ _____

(어떤 일이* / 이상한 / 일어났다 / 그에게)

B 주어진 단어들을 활용하여 단락을 완성하세요.

challenging 도전적인	enjoy 즐기다	give 주다
hear 듣다	last month 지난달	life 인생
special 특별한	unbelievable 믿을 수 없는	yesterday 어제

1 _____. She sometimes takes
   (Veronica는 / 즐긴다 / (어떤) 것을 / 도전적인)   가끔   참여하다

part in something dangerous. _____
                위험한   (어제 / 나는 / 들었다 / (어떤) 것을 /

_____. She went bungee jumping.
    믿을 수 없는)

2 _____. It was a
   (Ray는 / 주었다 / 내게 / (어떤) 것을 / 특별한 / 지난달에)

puppy. It was little and cute. _____
  강아지   귀여운   (그것은 / 되었다 / (어떤) 것이 / 중요한 /

_____.
   내 인생에서)

C 그림을 묘사해 보세요.

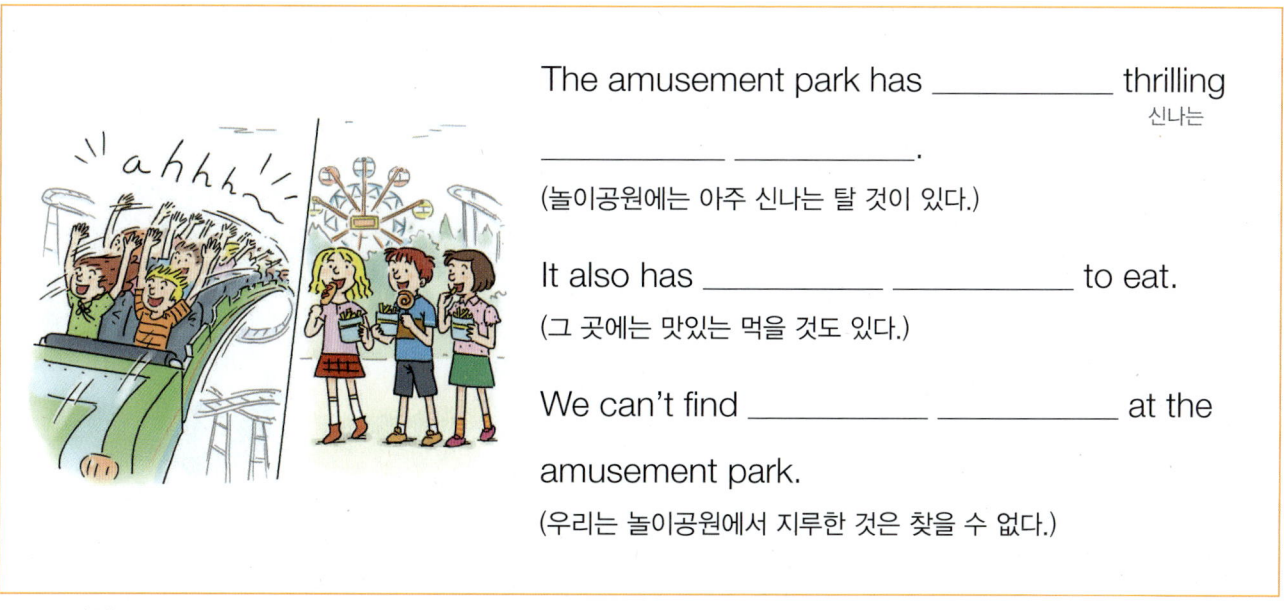

The amusement park has _____ thrilling
                                      신나는
_____ _____.
(놀이공원에는 아주 신나는 탈 것이 있다.)

It also has _____ _____ to eat.
(그 곳에는 맛있는 먹을 것도 있다.)

We can't find _____ _____ at the

amusement park.
(우리는 놀이공원에서 지루한 것은 찾을 수 없다.)

* 주요 어휘는 Word Test p.117에서 한 번 더 연습하세요.

Review 04 Journal

A 아래 표를 참고하여, 나의 장래 희망에 대한 글에 들어갈 내용을 정리하세요.

What I Want to Be	Reasons 이유(들)
scientist	• am interested in anything scientific 　~에 흥미가 있다　　　　과학적인 • want to invent something good for people 　　　　발명하다 • enjoy working on a team

OUTLINE

Title   What I Want to Be

Beginning   I want to be a scientist.
　　　　　　　　　　　　　　　과학자

Middle   - am interested in _____ _____; like to read science books and magazines
　　　　　　　　　　　　　　　　　　　　　　　　　　　잡지들
　　　　　- want _____ _____ _____ _____ for people; hope to help people with it
　　　　　- enjoy _____ _____ _____ _____; want to be a member of a research group
　　　　　　　　　　　　　　　　　　　　　　　　　　연구

Ending   My teacher advises me to study hard.

---

invent 발명하다　　　research 연구　　　scientific 과학적인

B 아웃라인을 바탕으로 나의 장래 희망에 대한 글을 완성하세요.

What I Want to Be — Title

I would like to tell you about what I want to be. I _____
~하기를 원하여
_____. ⎤ Beginning

There are some reasons for that. First, I am _____
_____. I like _____ and magazines.

Second, I want _____.
I hope to _____. I think helping others is something wonderful.
아주 멋진/훌륭한

Last, I enjoy _____. I heard scientists usually work together. I _____ of a research group.
함께

My teacher _____ to be a scientist. I will try to do my best. ⎤ Ending
최선

Middle

아래 내용을 모두 잘 학습하였으면 □안에 ✔하세요.

☐ to부정사나 동명사(-ing : ~하는 것)를 목적어로 취하는 동사를 맞게 사용하였다.

☐ 목적어 뒤에 to부정사를 사용하였다.

☐ -thing 뒤에 수식어구(형용사)를 붙여 맞게 사용하였다.

Unit 13 과거분사 만들기

Part 1 Grammar Point

A 규칙동사의 과거분사는 아래와 같이 만듭니다. 외우지 않아도 됩니다. 영어공부를 꾸준히 하다보면 저절로 알아집니다.

규칙동사	규 칙	예 시
대부분의 동사	+ ed	• cook: cook + ed → cook**ed** • walk: walk + ed → walk**ed**
-e로 끝나는 동사	-e + d	• change: chang**e** + d → chang**ed** • smile: smil**e** + d → smil**ed**
자음+-y로 끝나는 동사	자음 + -yi + ed	• study: stud**yi** + ed → stud**ied**
모음+-y로 끝나는 동사	모음 + -y + ed	• play: pla**y** + ed → pla**yed**
단모음+단자음 동사	끝자음 + ed	• plan: plan + **n** + ed → plan**ned** • stop: stop + **p** + ed → stop**ped**

* 불규칙 변화 동사표는 과거분사는 Appendix p.108-109 참고

B 과거분사는 형용사처럼 명사를 수식합니다. 완료(~한)의 의미와 수동(~된)의 의미로 사용할 수 있습니다.

• I picked up the **fallen** leaves.　　　나는 떨어진 잎을 주웠다.

• Does he know the **changed** schedule?　그가 변경된 스케줄을 알고 있습니까?

* 과거분사를 명사 뒤로 보낸 후 다른 수식어와 함께 쓸 수 있습니다.

This is a house built years ago.　　　이것은 여러 해 전에 지어진 집이다.

Part 2 Grammar Exercise

A 다음 빈칸에 동사의 알맞은 과거분사형을 쓰세요.

1. walk → _____
2. shut 닫다 → _____
3. try → _____
4. change → _____
5. play → _____
6. forget 잊어버리다 → _____
7. dry 말리다 → _____
8. stop → _____
9. begin → _____
10. think → _____
11. invent 발명하다 → _____
12. give → _____

B ① 주어진 상황을 살펴보고 동사를 과거분사로 만드세요.

| wall 벽 | windows 창문(들) | paint 페인트 칠하다 | bake 굽다 | close 닫다 | potatoes 감자(들) |

② '과거분사 + 명사'를 사용해서 내용을 완성하세요.

1.  They like _____ _____.

2.  The family picture is on the _____ _____.

3.  The house with _____ _____ is mine. 나의 것

Unit 13 과거분사 만들기

C 동사들을 내용에 맞게 고쳐서 문장을 완성하세요.

respect	print	break	wash	update
존경하다	프린트하다	깨다	씻다	최근 정보를 알려주다

1 Please tell me _____ news about him.

2 The man brought his _____ clothes.
   가지고 왔다

3 The _____ police officer is Jerry.

4 She will pay for the _____ window.
   지불하다

5 The teacher handed out the _____ paper.
   나눠주었다

D 밑줄 친 부분을 올바른 과거분사 철자로 고쳐서 문장을 완성하세요.

> 보기 Don't throw away the breaked computer.
>   버리다
>   → Don't throw away the broken computer.

1 Our group took a guiden tour of Mexico.

  → Our group took a _____ tour of Mexico.

2 Jamie found the stoled watch.

  → Jamie found the _____ watch.

3 The ambulance arrived to take the injure people.
                    도착했다

  → The ambulance arrived to take the _____ people.

4 I bought a book wrote in English.
         샀다

  → I bought a book _____ in English.

MUST-HAVE 2

E 주어진 동사를 과거분사로 바꿔 알맞은 곳에 넣어 문장의 뜻을 확장하세요.

요리하다
1 I always try to eat only food. (cook)
→ _____

골랐다/꺾었다/집었다
2 Linda picked the flower. (fall)
→ _____

~판/버전   개설하다
3 We need a version of this game. (upgrade)
→ _____

고치다
4 Jack brought us a radio. (fix)
→ _____

초대하다
5 Many people to the party didn't come. (invite)
→ _____

F 주어진 단어들을 바르게 배열하여 문장을 완성하세요. (참고: 영어는 항상 '주어'를 먼저 찾아야 해요.)

털린/강도가 들어온
1 the robbed / arrived at / bank / The police
→ _____
(경찰이 강도가 들어온 은행에 도착했다.)

그려진/그린
2 The picture / looks good / drawn / by your sister
→ _____
(너의 여동생이 그린 그림은 훌륭해 보인다.)

~을 더 좋아하다   사용된/중고의
3 prefer to buy / books / Some students / used
→ _____
(일부 학생들은 중고 책을 구입하는 것을 선호한다.)

다친/부상당한   군인들
4 not enough doctors for / the wounded / There were / soldiers
→ _____
(부상당한 군인들을 위한 의사들이 충분하지 않았다.)

Unit 13 과거분사 만들기

Part 3 Writing Practice

A 주어진 단어들을 활용하여 문장을 영작하세요.

as a dessert 후식으로	break 부러지다	chair 의자	find 발견하다	freeze 얼다
heal 치료하다	leave 남기다	lock 잠그다	look for 찾다	lose 잃어버리다
near 근처에	parking lot 주차장	police 경찰	puppy 강아지	steal 훔치다
towel 수건	wing 날개	yogurt 요구르트		

1 나는 나의 잃어버린 강아지를 찾는 중이다.

→ _____

(나는 / 찾는 중이다 / 나의 잃어버린 강아지를)

2 의자 위에 남겨진 그 수건은 나의 것이다.

→ _____

(그 수건은 / 남겨진 / 의자 위에 / 이다 / 나의 것)

3 그녀는 날개가 부러진 새를 치료했다.

→ _____

(그녀는 / 치료했다 / 새를 / 부러진 날개를 가진)

4 Tina는 후식으로 얼린 요구르트를 좋아한다.

→ _____

(Tina는 / 좋아한다 / 얼린 요구르트를 / 후식으로)

5 경찰은 주차장 근처에서 도난 당한 차를 발견했다.

→ _____

(경찰은 / 발견했다 / 도난 당한 차를 / 근처에서 / 주차장)

6 Alice는 큰 열쇠로 그 잠긴 문을 열었다.

→ _____

(Alice는 / 열었다 / 그 잠긴 문을 / 큰 열쇠로)

MUST-HAVE 2

B 주어진 단어들을 활용하여 단락을 완성하세요.

| accident 사고 | cause 일으키다 | drink 술을 마시다 | driver 운전자 | German 독일어 |
| hit 치다 | name ~라고 부르다 | smart 똑똑한 | write 쓰다 | |

1 A: Did you see the accident? How did it happen?
     　　　　　　　　　　사고　　　　　　　　일어나다/발생하다

   B: Yes, _____. I think _____
          (나는 / 보았다 / 그 소년을 / 치인 / 차에)   (술을 마신 /

   _____.
   운전자가 / 일으켰다 / 그 사고를)

2 _____. She can speak four
   (나의 친구는 / ~라고 불리는 / Jody / 이다 / 매우 똑똑한)

   languages. In particular, _____
   언어들   특히/특별히   (그녀는 / 좋아한다 / 책을 읽는 것을 / 쓰인 /

   _____.
   독일어로)

C 그림을 묘사해 보세요.

　　　　　　　　　　　　　　　　안내문/게시물
A: Did you see the notice _____ on the board? (게시판에 게시된 알림 봤니?)

B: Yes, I heard that many _____
　　　　　　　　　　　　　　신청했다
_____ applied for the contest.
(응, 많은 재능 있는 학생들이 신청했다고 들었어.)
　　　　　　괜찮은　　　　따르다
A: You will do fine if you follow the _____

_____, too.
(주어진 지시사항을 따르면 너도 잘 할거야.)

＊ 주요 어휘는 Word Test p.118에서 한 번 더 연습하세요.

Unit 14 수동태

Part 1 Grammar Point

A 능동태는 주어가 동작의 주체가 되고, 수동태는 주어가 동작을 '받거나 당하는' 대상이 됩니다.

능동 → **수동**

- The repairman **fixed** the computer. → The computer **was fixed** by the repairman.
  그 수리공이 그 컴퓨터를 고쳤다. 그 컴퓨터는 그 수리공에 의해 고쳐졌다.

- My father **drew** the picture. → The picture **was drawn** by my father.
  나의 아버지가 그 그림을 그렸다. 그 그림은 나의 아버지에 의해 그려졌다.

B 수동태는 [주어 + be동사 + 과거분사 + by 행위자]로 문장을 완성하면 됩니다.

> 주어 + **be**동사 + 과거분사 + by 행위자

- 능동태: The reporter wrote the article. 그 기자가 그 기사를 썼다.
- 수동태: The article was written by the reporter. 그 기사는 그 기자에 의해 쓰였다.

* by 행위자는 일반인이거나 알 수 없는 경우 또는 중요하지 않을 때 생략할 수 있습니다.

C 수동태의 be동사로 시제를 원하는 대로 바꿀 수 있습니다.

- **과거** The telephone was invented by Bell. 전화기는 Bell에 의해 발명되었다.
- **현재** All of the windows are closed. 모든 창문들이 닫혀 있다.
- **미래** The book will be published soon. 그 책은 곧 출판될 것이다.

Part 2 Grammar Exercise

A ① 다음 주어진 동사를 과거분사의 형태로 바꾸세요.

hold → _____,   speak → _____,   serve → _____
열리다, 개최하다   말하다   제공하다

② 주어진 상황을 설명하기 위해서 수동태를 사용하세요.

1  Chinese is _____ in China.

2  Dinner will be _____ in a minute.
　　　　　　　　　　　　　　　　　　　　　　　즉시/곧

3  The Olympic Games are _____ every four years.
　　　　　　　　　　　　　　　　　　　　　　　　　　　매/마다

B 밑줄 친 주어가 동작을 하면 '능동', 동작을 받으면 '수동'이라고 쓰세요.

1 <u>Spaghetti</u> will be served soon.　　　　　　　　　_____

2 <u>The guards</u> open the gate every morning.　　　_____

3 <u>Some of my friends</u> are invited to the party.　_____

4 <u>The invention</u> was made in Korea in 2008.　　_____
　　발명품

5 <u>The orchestra</u> made beautiful sounds.　　　　 _____

Unit 14 수동태

C '주어' 입장에서 볼 때 내용상 가장 적절한 표현을 고르세요.

1 People (polluted / are polluted) many rivers.
   오염시켰다

2 The problem (caused / was caused) by Jimmy.
   발생했다

3 The pictures (took / were taken) by David.
   사진 찍었다

4 He (will be announced / will announce) the news tomorrow.
   발표했다

5 The bread (was baked / baked) by my mother yesterday.
   구웠다

D 밑줄 친 부분을 올바르게 고쳐서 내용을 완성하세요.

> 보기 The bicycle fix by me yesterday.
> → The bicycle was fixed by me yesterday.

1 James born in Chicago.
   태어난

   → James _____ in Chicago.

2 The music will play by the orchestra.

   → The music will _____ by the orchestra.

3 The street blocked by the police last month.
   막았다

   → The street _____ by the police last month.

4 The ceremony was host by actor James Harris last year.
   의식/예식/행사 주최하다 배우

   → The ceremony _____ by actor James Harris last year.

E 목적어를 주어로 사용해서 '수동태' 문장을 만드세요.

1 Tom wrote the essay. (글/에세이, 목적어)
→ _____

2 Steven cleaned his room. (목적어)
→ _____

3 People destroy many forests. (숲, 목적어)
→ _____

4 My uncle fixed the broken computer. (목적어)
→ _____

5 Henry canceled the meeting yesterday. (취소했다, 목적어)
→ _____

F 주어진 단어들을 바르게 배열하여 문장을 완성하세요.(참고:영어는 항상 '주어*'를 먼저 찾아야 해요.)

1 was painted / last week / The building wall* (벽)
→ _____
(그 건물 벽은 지난주에 페인트칠해졌다.)

2 by the police / The thief* / was arrested
→ _____
(그 도둑은 경찰에 의해 체포되었다.)

3 are loved / Cartoons* / by many children
→ _____
(만화는 많은 어린이들에 의해 사랑받는다.)

4 was written / a year ago / The story* / by Dan
→ _____
(그 이야기는 Dan에 의해 1년 전에 쓰였다.)

Unit 14 수동태

Part 3 Writing Practice

A 주어진 단어들을 활용하여 문장을 영작하세요.

brother 남동생	cucumber 오이	drop 떨어지다	everybody 모두
fix 고치다	grow 재배하다	in a moment 순식간에	in the backyard 뒤뜰에서
love 사랑하다	machine 기계	many 많은	on the floor 바닥에
sell out 다 팔다	sing (노래) 부르다	teenager 십대	ticket 표

1 그 표들은 순식간에 다 팔렸다.

→ _____

(그 표들은 / 다 팔렸다 / 순식간에)

2 이 오이들은 뒤뜰에서 재배되었다.

→ _____

(이 오이들은 / 재배되었다 / 뒤뜰에서)

3 그 기계는 Tim에 의해 고쳐졌다.

→ _____

(그 기계는 / 고쳐졌다 / Tim에 의해)

4 그 컵은 내 남동생에 의해 바닥에 떨어졌다.

→ _____

(그 컵은 / 떨어졌다 / 바닥에 / 내 남동생에 의해)

5 Angela는 모두에게 사랑받는다.

→ _____

(Angela는 / 사랑받는다 / 모두에게)

6 이 노래는 많은 십대들에게 불려진다.

→ _____

(이 노래는 / 불려진다 / 많은 십대들에게)

B 주어진 단어들을 활용하여 단락을 완성하세요.

| a week ago 일주일 전에 | bike 자전거 | country 나라 | famous 유명한 | in English 영어로 |
| keep 보관하다 | speak 말하다 | thief 도둑 | usually 주로 | yard 마당 |

1 _____. It was a gift
      (나의 자전거는 / 도난당했다 / 도둑에게 / 일주일 전에)   선물

from my father. _____. It is
~로 부터   (그것은 / 주로 / 보관되었다 / 마당에)

strange because my bicycle was always locked.
이상한/의아한   잠긴/잠겨진

2 English is a global language. _____.
      세계적인/지구의   (영어는 / 말해진다 / 많은 나라들에서)

_____.
(많은 / 유명한 책들이 / 쓰인다 / 영어로)

English is also used on useful websites.
                              유용한

C 그림을 묘사해 보세요.

before

after

A new gym will _____ _____ in our school. (우리 학교에 새로운 체육관이 지어질 것이다.)

The old place _____ _____ _____ to a new gym.
(그 낡은 공간은 새 체육관으로 바뀔 것이다.)

And, it _____ _____ _____ by many P.E. lovers.
(그리고 체육을 사랑하는 많은 사람들에 의해 사용될 것이다.)

* P.E. = physical education 의 준말

* 주요 어휘는 Word Test p.118에서 한 번 더 연습하세요.

Unit 15 부정대명사

Part 1 Grammar Point

A -body / -one은 **부정대명사**의 하나로서 **불특정한 사람**을 가리킵니다. 항상 단수 취급합니다.

부정대명사	쓰 임	의 미	예 문
somebody (someone)	평서문	누군가	• **Someone** asked me the way to the station. 누군가 내게 역으로 가는 길을 물었다.
	의문문 (권유, 부탁의 경우)	누구	• Will **somebody** answer the door, please? 누구 문 좀 열어주시겠어요?
anybody (anyone)	평서문	누구라도, 아무나	• It is free. **Anyone** can have it. 그것은 무료이다. 누구라도 그것을 가질 수 있다.
	부정문	아무도	• There wasn't **anyone** in the room. 방에는 아무도 없었다. • I didn't tell **anyone** about the secret. 나는 그 비밀에 대해 아무에게도 말하지 않았다.
	의문문	누구	• Is there **anybody** inside the house? 그 집 안에 누구 있나요?
nobody (no one)	모든 문장 형식	아무도 (누구도) ~않다	• **No one** can predict the future. 누구도 미래를 예측할 수 없다. • There was **nobody** in the office. 사무실에는 아무도 없었다.

Part 2 Grammar Exercise

A 가장 자연스러운 부정대명사를 사용해서 주어진 상황을 설명하세요.

| somebody | anybody | nobody |

1. _____ can solve the problem.
   풀다   문제

2. I didn't expect _____ today.
   기대하다

3. _____ helped me the other day.
   지난 번/며칠 전에

B 주어가 부정대명사일 때 문법적으로 올바른 쓰임을 고르세요.

1. Someone (is / are) knocking on the door.

2. Nobody (like / likes) to lose the game.
   잃다/지다

3. (Do / Does) anyone have a question?

4. No one (is / are) too old to learn.
   나이많은

5. Someone (want / wants) to talk to you.
   얘기하다

Unit 15 부정대명사

C 내용상 가장 적절한 부정대명사를 골라 문장을 완성하세요.

| someone | anybody | no one |

1 Please wait. _____ will visit you to fix the roof.

2 I feel scared. I can't see _____ around here.

3 Can you keep it a secret? _____ should know the truth.

4 I need to study French. Do you know _____ who speaks French?

5 I hear _____ singing a song. I like the song.

D 부정대명사가 사용된 문장을 올바르게 해석하세요.

1 Someone called you this morning.
→ _____

2 Anyone can succeed if he/she tries hard.
→ _____

3 No one complained about the plan.
→ _____

4 Helping someone will make you happy.
→ _____

5 Nobody came to the party.
→ _____

E 밑줄 친 부분을 바르게 고쳐서 문장을 완성하세요.

> 보기 Will <u>nobody</u> help me move this box?
> 　　　　　　　　　　　옮기다
> → Will somebody help me move this box?

1　<u>Anybody</u> asked me for my telephone number.

　→ _____ asked me for my telephone number.

2　I didn't see <u>no one</u> in the gym.

　→ I didn't see _____ in the gym.

3　Sadly, <u>anyone</u> found my wallet yesterday.
　　　　　　　　　　　　　　남자 지갑
　→ Sadly, _____ found my wallet yesterday.

4　I don't know <u>someone</u> called Pamela.

　→ I don't know _____ called Pamela.

F 주어진 단어들을 바르게 배열하여 문장을 완성하세요. (참고: 영어는 항상 '주어'를 먼저 찾아야 해요.)

1　can go / Anybody / to public school

　→ _____
　　(누구나 공립학교에 갈 수 있다.)

2　while / called / Somebody / you were out

　→ _____
　　(누군가 네가 나간 동안 전화를 했다.)

3　at / There is / Somebody / the front door

　→ _____
　　(누군가 현관문 앞에 있다.)

4　enough to / Nobody / was brave / save the girl

　→ _____
　　(아무도 그 소녀를 구할 만큼 충분히 용감하지 않았다.)

Unit 15 부정대명사

Part 3 Writing Practice

A 주어진 단어들을 활용하여 문장을 영작하세요.

artist 예술가	be willing to 기꺼이 ~하다	easy 쉬운	explain 설명하다
game 게임	in this area 이 지역의	know 알다	need 필요하다
problem 문제	should ~해야 한다	story 이야기	take a risk 위험을 무릅쓰다
take care of 해결하다	understand 이해하다		

1 누군가 그 문제를 해결해야 한다.

→ _____

(누군가 / 해야 한다 / 해결하다 / 그 문제를)

2 나는 이 지역의 아무도 몰랐다. (anyone)

→ _____

(나는 / 몰랐다 / 아무도 / 이 지역의)

3 아무도 기꺼이 그 위험을 무릅쓰려 하지 않는다. (no one)

→ _____

(아무도 ~않다 / 기꺼이 ~하다 / 위험을 무릅쓰려)

4 아무도 그가 유명한 예술가라는 것을 몰랐다. (nobody)

→ _____

(아무도 ~않다 / 알았다 / 그가 / 이었다 / 유명한 예술가라는 것을)

5 누구나 그 쉬운 게임을 이해할 수 있다.

→ _____

(누구나 / 이해할 수 있다 / 그 쉬운 게임을)

6 나는 이 이야기를 설명해줄 누군가가 필요하다.

→ _____

(나는 / 필요하다 / 누군가가 / 설명해줄 / 이 이야기를)

B 주어진 단어들을 활용하여 단락을 완성하세요.

| anywhere 어디에서도 | call 부르다 | except 제외하고 | hear 듣다 |
| name 이름 | rat 쥐 | some 몇몇 | there 거기서 |

1 Jeff and I had different stories to tell. Jeff told me that he saw someone in the
   다른

   basement. But _____.
   지하층(실)   (나는 / 보지 못했다 / 아무도 / 거기서)

   _____ (There was ~).
   (있었다 / 아무도 ~않다 (nobody) / 제외하고 / 몇 마리 쥐들을)

2 _____. I opened the
   (나는 / 들었다 / 누군가 / 부르는 / 내 이름을)

   window and looked outside. But _____
   밖을 바라보았다   (나는 / 볼 수 없었다 / 아무도 /

   _____.
   어디에서도)

C 그림을 묘사해 보세요.

찾는
A: Are you looking for _____?
   (누군가를 찾고 있나요?)

B: Yes. Is there _____ who can help us

   find the library?
   (네. 우리가 도서관 찾는 것을 도와줄 누가 있나요?)

A: Oh, I know _____ who can _____

   _____. Please wait.
   (아, 여러분을 도와줄 누군가를 내가 알아요. 잠시만 기다리세요.)

* 주요 어휘는 Word Test p.119에서 한 번 더 연습하세요.

Review 05 — Descriptive Essay

A 아래 그림과 단어박스를 참고하여, 교실 상황을 묘사하는 글에 들어갈 내용을 정리하세요.

OUTLINE

Title What Happened in This Classroom?
　　　　　　　　　　　　　일어났다/발생했다

Beginning something must have happened in the classroom yesterday
　　　　　　　　　　　　　　　　　　　～임에 틀림없다

Middle
Closed Window: _____ _____ → no one answers
　　　　　　닫힌

Desk: is stained with ink → _____ _____ says who did that
　　　　　　　　　얼룩진

Blackboard: _____ _____ _____ scribbles → _____ will
　　　　　　　　칠판　　　　　　　　　　　　　　　낙서하다/낙서

answer

Ending Who did all these things?
　　　　　　　　　했다　　이러한

＊ be stained with ～로 얼룩지다   scribble 낙서

be broken	be filled with	nobody	no one
깨졌다	～로 가득찼다	아무도 ～않다	아무도 ～않다

B 아웃라인을 바탕으로 그림을 묘사하는 에세이를 완성하세요.

What Happened in This Classroom? — Title

I think something must have happened _____
_____. ⎤ Beginning

The _____ window _____. The teacher asks
who broke the window, but _____.
     깼다
We need to find out who did that. In addition, the desk _____
       찾아내다   게다가
_____. Somebody may have dropped an ink bottle on
                             떨어뜨렸다   병
the desk, but _____ says who did that. I can also see the
                                                  또한
blackboard _____. Who did it? Maybe ⎦ Middle
_____.

Who on earth did all these things? — Ending
도대체

✏️ 아래 내용을 모두 잘 학습하였으면 □안에 ✔하세요.

☐ 과거분사(broken, filed, colsed, stained)를 사용하여 완료 · 수동의 의미를 표현하였다.

☐ 수동태(be동사 + 과거분사)를 올바르게 사용하였다.

☐ 부정대명사(nobody, no one, somebody)로 불특정한 사람을 표현하였다.

Appendix

불규칙 변화 동사표

A-A-A형

원 형	과 거	과거분사	원 형	과 거	과거분사
cut	cut	cut	read	read	read
hurt	hurt	hurt	set	set	set
let	let	let	shut	shut	shut
put	put	put			

A-B-A형

원 형	과 거	과거분사	원 형	과 거	과거분사
become	became	become	run	ran	run
come	came	come			

A-B-B형

원 형	과 거	과거분사	원 형	과 거	과거분사
bend	bent	bent	hold	held	held
bring	brought	brought	keep	kept	kept
build	built	built	lay	laid	laid
burn	burned/burnt	burned/burnt	lead	led	led
buy	bought	bought	leave	left	left
catch	caught	caught	lend	lent	lent
dive	dived/dove	dived	lose	lost	lost
feed	fed	fed	slide	slid	slid
feel	felt	felt	speed	sped/speeded	sped/speeded
fight	fought	fought	spend	spent	spent
find	found	found	stand	stood	stood
get	got	gotten/got	make	made	made
hang	hung	hung	mean	meant	meant
have	had	had	meet	met	met
hear	heard	heard	pay	paid	paid

108

원형	과거	과거분사	원형	과거	과거분사
say	said	said	strike	struck	struck/stricken
sell	sold	sold	teach	taught	taught
send	sent	sent	tell	told	told
shine	shone	shone	think	thought	thought
sit	sat	sat	understand	understood	understood
sleep	slept	slept	win	won	won

A-B-C형

원형	과거	과거분사	원형	과거	과거분사
awake	awoke	awoken	know	knew	known
be	was/were	been	lie	lay	lain
begin	began	begun	ride	rode	ridden
blow	blew	blown	ring	rang	rung
break	broke	broken	see	saw	seen
choose	chose	chosen	shake	shook	shaken
do	did	done	show	showed	shown
draw	drew	drawn	sing	sang	sung
drink	drank	drunk	sink	sank	sunk
drive	drove	driven	speak	spoke	spoken
eat	ate	eaten	spring	sprang	sprung
fall	fell	fallen	steal	stole	stolen
fly	flew	flown	swim	swam	swum
forget	forgot	forgotten	take	took	taken
forgive	forgave	forgiven	throw	threw	thrown
freeze	froze	frozen	wake	woke	woken
give	gave	given	wear	wore	worn
go	went	gone	write	wrote	written
grow	grew	grown			

Appendix

to부정사를 목적어로 취하는 동사 모음

동사	뜻	동사	뜻
advise him to	그에게 ~할 것을 충고하다	hesitate to	~하는 것을 망설이다
afford to	~할 여유/여력이 있다	hope to	~할 것을 희망하다
agree to	~할 것을 동의하다	instruct to	~할 것을 교육하다/가르치다
allow to	~할 것을 허락하다	learn to	~하는 것을 배우다
arrange to	~할 것을 마련하다, 주선하다	manage to	~하는 것을 관리하다
ask to	~할 것을 요청하다	mean to	~하는 것을 뜻하다
attempt to	~할 것을 시도하다	need to	~하는 것이 필요하다
beg to	~할 것을 (간절히) 부탁하다	offer to	~할 것을 제공하다/제안하다
bother to	~하는 것을 방해하다	order to	~할 것을 명령하다
care to	~하는 것에 관심을 가지다, 배려하다	persuade to	~할 것을 설득하다
cause to	~하는 것을 야기하다	plan to	~할 것을 준비하다
challenge to	~하는 것을/에 도전하다	prepare to	~하는 척하다
claim to	~하는 것을 주장하다	promise to	~할 것을 약속하다
decide to	~할 것을 결심하다	refuse to	~할 것을 거절하다
demand to	~할 것을 요구하다	regret to	~할 것을 유감스러워하다/후회하다
deserve to	~할 자격이 있다	reject to	~할 것을 거절하다
encourage to	~할 것을 격려하다/용기를 북돋아 주다	remember to	~할 것을 기억하다
expect to	~할 것을 기대하다	rush to	~할 것을 서두르다
fail to	~하는 것을 실패하다	seem to	~할 것처럼 보인다/~할 것 같다
force to	~할 것을 강요하다	struggle to	~하는 것을 고군분투하다
forget to	~할 것을 잊어버리다	swear to	~할 것을 맹세하다
teach to	~하는 것을 가르치다		

Word Test
Book 2

MUST-HAVE Grammar

Word Test

■ 다음 단어를 영어는 한글로, 한글은 영어로 바꿔 쓰시오.

Unit 01 정답 pp. 12-13

1. apartment _____
2. hear _____
3. here _____
4. parcel _____
5. room _____
6. 매일 _____
7. 지금 _____
8. ~값을 지불하다 _____
9. ~에 관해 _____
10. ~에 살다 _____

Unit 02 정답 pp. 18-19

1. at night _____
2. fight with _____
3. get in _____
4. restaurant _____
5. today _____
6. 거짓말하다 _____
7. 비싼 _____
8. 비용이 들다 _____
9. 수영하다 _____
10. 제공하다 _____

■ 다음 단어를 영어는 한글로, 한글은 영어로 바꿔 쓰시오.

Unit 03 정답 pp. 24-25

1 air _____

2 clean _____

3 enough _____

4 machine _____

5 take a walk _____

6 목소리 _____

7 소리가 큰 _____

8 신선한 _____

9 실수를 하다 _____

10 ~을 보살피다 _____

Unit 04 정답 pp. 32-33

1 announce _____

2 future _____

3 part _____

4 return _____

5 trip _____

6 다음의 _____

7 부르다 _____

8 생각하다 _____

9 영웅 _____

10 (여성용) 지갑 _____

■ 다음 단어를 영어는 한글로, 한글은 영어로 바꿔 쓰시오.

Unit 05 정답 pp. 38-39

1. buy _____
2. dinner _____
3. nervous _____
4. tennis _____
5. yesterday _____
6. 묻다 _____
7. 시작하다 _____
8. 시합 _____
9. 실험 _____
10. 표 _____

Unit 06 정답 pp. 44-45

1. always _____
2. bike _____
3. cafeteria _____
4. need _____
5. stay healthy _____
6. 가져오다 _____
7. 쓰레기 _____
8. 연구하다 _____
9. 타다 _____
10. 확인하다 _____

■ 다음 단어를 영어는 한글로, 한글은 영어로 바꿔 쓰시오.

Unit 07   정답 pp. 52-53

1. bitter _____
2. medicine _____
3. poor _____
4. warm _____
5. wild _____
6. 간단한 _____
7. 그림 _____
8. 다루다 _____
9. 먹이를 주다 _____
10. 멀리 떨어진 _____

Unit 08   정답 pp. 58-59

1. adult _____
2. England _____
3. fix _____
4. spend _____
5. this _____
6. 소설 _____
7. 수리공 _____
8. 아이들 _____
9. 일 _____
10. 조언 _____

■ 다음 단어를 영어는 한글로, 한글은 영어로 바꿔 쓰시오.

Unit 09 정답 pp.64-65

1 at the door _____

2 dream _____

3 in front of _____

4 report _____

5 understand _____

6 가입하다 _____

7 믿다 _____

8 소식 _____

9 이루어지다 _____

10 진실 _____

Unit 10 정답 pp.72-73

1 do volunteer work _____

2 everyone _____

3 invite _____

4 light _____

5 there _____

6 끄다 _____

7 다른 사람들 _____

8 당분간 _____

9 평화를 유지하다 _____

10 함께 _____

MUST-HAVE 2

■ 다음 단어를 영어는 한글로, 한글은 영어로 바꿔 쓰시오.

Unit 11   정답 pp. 78-79

1 bank   _____

2 fat   _____

3 run a race   _____

4 skip meals   _____

5 stay up   _____

6 과학자   _____

7 너무 많은   _____

8 되다   _____

9 작가   _____

10 저축하다   _____

Unit 12   정답 pp. 84-85

1 creative   _____

2 invention   _____

3 old man   _____

4 special   _____

5 wrong   _____

6 놀라운   _____

7 도전적인   _____

8 마술   _____

9 믿을 수 없는   _____

10 ~에게 일어나다 _____

■ 다음 단어를 영어는 한글로, 한글은 영어로 바꿔 쓰시오.

Unit 13   정답 pp. 92-93

1. break _____
2. heal _____
3. lock _____
4. parking lot _____
5. steal _____
6. 경찰 _____
7. 얼다 _____
8. 의자 _____
9. 일으키다 _____
10. 잃어버리다 _____

Unit 14   정답 pp. 98-99

1. cucumber _____
2. drop _____
3. in a moment _____
4. sell out _____
5. usually _____
6. 도둑 _____
7. 바닥에 _____
8. 십대 _____
9. 유명한 _____
10. 재배하다 _____

■ 다음 단어를 영어는 한글로, 한글은 영어로 바꿔 쓰시오.

Unit 15 정답 pp.104-105

1 anywhere _____

2 artist _____

3 easy _____

4 game _____

5 take a risk _____

6 기꺼이 ~하다 _____

7 문제 _____

8 설명하다 _____

9 제외하고 _____

10 해결하다 _____

Answer Key Book 2

MUST-HAVE Grammar

Answer Key

Unit 01

Grammar Exercise pp. 09-11

A

1. Did / open
2. Do / have
3. Does / like / does

B

1. Did
2. Do
3. Does
4. Did
5. Does

C

1. lock
2. sell
3. turn
4. enjoy

D

1. Does / Sam / like
2. Do / they / walk
3. Did / it / rain
4. Did / Andy / lose

E

1. Q: Does Jenny like the new CD?
   A: Yes, she does.
2. Q: Did Hank find the solution to the problem?
   A: Yes, he did.
3. Q: Did they give you a birthday card?
   A: No, they did not. OR
      No, they didn't.
4. Q: Do you drive your own car?
   A: Yes, I do.

F

1. Did Tom fall off his bike?
2. Does Mr. Joshua teach art?
3. Do we have any homework?
4. Does it snow in Africa?

Writing Practice pp. 12-13

A

1. Did you get my parcel?
2. Does Tony come here?
3. Do they live in an apartment?
4. Did we pay for the food?
5. Do you eat breakfast every day?
6. Did you clean your room?

B

1. Did you hear about Keith /
   No, he did not OR
   No, he didn't
2. Does she have many friends now /
   Yes, she does

C

Did / you / go
Yes / I / did
Did / you / see
Yes / I / did

Unit 02

Grammar Exercise pp. 15-17

A

don't / doesn't / didn't

1. didn't / eat
2. don't / go
3. doesn't / sleep

B

1. doesn't
2. don't
3. doesn't
4. didn't
5. didn't

C

1. know
2. take
3. give
4. have

D

1. ② ① ③
2. ③ ② ①
3. ② ① ③
4. ① ③ ②

E

1. didn't / help
2. doesn't / sell
3. don't / wear
4. doesn't / ask

F

1. Tim did not wait for me.
2. I don't live in the dormitory.
3. She does not speak clearly.
4. The restaurant doesn't open until 11 a.m.

Writing Practice pp. 18-19

A

1. Jeremy did not get in a car. OR
   Jeremy didn't get in a car.
2. I do not go jogging on the weekend. OR
   I don't go jogging on the weekend.
3. My mother does not watch TV at night. OR
   My mother doesn't watch TV at night.
4. Sarah does not want an expensive gift. OR
   Sarah doesn't want an expensive gift.
5. Naomi did not swim in the sea. OR
   Naomi didn't swim in the sea.
6. He did not miss the school bus today. OR
   He didn't miss the school bus today.

B

1. I do not lie to my friends OR
   I don't lie to my friends /
   I do not fight with them OR
   I don't fight with them
2. The restaurant does not serve junk food OR
   The restaurant doesn't serve junk food /
   the restaurant does not cost a lot OR
   the restaurant doesn't cost a lot

C

doesn't / snow
don't / wear
don't / walk
don't / eat

Unit 03
Grammar Exercise pp. 21-23

A

1. do / look
2. does / smell
3. did / brush

B

1. do
2. does
3. did
4. did
5. do

Answer Key

C

1. wash
2. go
3. want
4. find
5. look

D

1. make
2. have
3. rain
4. like
5. take

E

1. I do study a lot before the exam.
2. The child does sleep alone every night.
3. He did come to school yesterday.
4. Nancy does speak French fluently.
5. My sister did make pasta for me.

F

1. I did go to the hospital.
2. Jack does have special talents.
3. We do know the truth.
4. They did run a lot on the playground.

Writing Practice pp. 24-25

A

1. I do take a walk on Saturdays.
2. Your uncle does have a loud voice.
3. I do remember your phone number.
4. Lenny did make a big mistake.
5. We do have enough time.
6. James did make a new machine.

B

1. I do like rainy days /
   Rain does give us clean and fresh air
2. we did have a good(great) time /
   He did care for me

C

do / look

did / study

do / hope

Review 01 pp. 26-27

A

do / like

don't / like

does / like / doesn't / like

do / like / don't / like

B

does like hamburgers

does not like cucumbers OR

doesn't like cucumbers

do like hamburgers

did like

do like meat

do not like vegetables OR

don't like vegetables

does like music

does not like math OR

doesn't like math

do like music

do not like science OR

don't like science

Do you

Unit 04
Grammar Exercise pp. 29-31

A

his   him   she   they

1. his
2. They
3. She / him

B

1. her
2. We
3. his
4. yours
5. me

C

1. her
2. him
3. theirs

D

1. We / them
2. He / she / hers
3. theirs
4. He / us

E

1. their / Ours
2. his / it
3. your / mine
4. her / Jake's

F

1. I enjoy talking with them.
2. We didn't understand her idea.
3. I think these shoes are his.
4. He told me to stand by her.

Writing Practice pp. 32-33

A

1. He calls his father a hero.
2. I think (that) the purse is hers.
3. Nick read his part, and I read mine.
4. We can't tell our futures.
5. Mike just returned from his trip.
6. He announced a new school rule to us.

B

1. my mother does not buy it for me OR
   my mother doesn't buy it for me /
   I am waiting for my next birthday OR
   I'm waiting for my next birthday
2. Gary is my best friend OR
   Gary's my best friend /
   I play soccer with him

C

you / your

it

I / you

I / your / pencil

Unit 05

Grammar Exercise pp. 35-37

A

1. Why
2. What
3. Who

B

1. Where
2. What
3. How
4. Where
5. When

C

1. invite
2. play
3. tell
4. go

Answer Key

D
1. What
2. How
3. Who
4. When
5. How

E
1. (2) (1) (3)
2. (1) (4) (3) (2)
3. (2) (1) (3) (4)
4. (3) (2) (4) (1)

F
1. When is your next taekwondo lesson?
2. Why are you so late?
3. Where do you play soccer?
4. What did you do last Sunday?

Writing Practice pp. 38-39

A
1. Why are they so nervous?
2. Where did you buy the ticket?
3. When does David eat dinner?
4. Who(Whom) did she see yesterday?
5. When do you start the experiment?
6. How did she win the tennis match?

B
1. Where did Mary go last weekend / Why do you ask
2. What should I buy for my parents / Where can I buy

C
How / can / I
What / did / you
Where / is

Unit 06

Grammar Exercise pp. 41-43

A
1. to / go
2. to / buy
3. to / do

B
1. in order to lose
2. to learn
3. to be late
4. to examine
5. to forget

C
1. in / order / to / stay / healthy
2. to / buy / some / juice
3. to / see / the / ancient / pyramids
4. to / arrive / on / time

D
1. not to forget
2. not to miss
3. in order not to waste
4. in order not to catch

E
1. I call him to say hello.
2. She will study harder to pass the exam.
3. He raised his hand to ask a question.
4. They went to bed early to wake up early in the morning.

F
1. I opened the window to get fresh air.
2. Linda tried hard not to laugh.
3. We practiced a lot in order to win the contest.
4. I walked carefully not to break the glass.

Writing Practice pp. 44-45

A

1. I brought the mop to clean the classroom.
2. Jessie opened the curtains to get enough sunlight.
3. Michelle went to the cafeteria to eat lunch.
4. She always wears a watch to check the time.
5. I took out the trash to help my mom.
6. What do I need to go to America?

B

1. She goes to a bookstore to buy fashion magazines /
   She needs them to study fashion trends
2. My dad rides his bike to stay healthy /
   My brother rides his bike to go to school

C

Why / do / you / study
in / order / to / talk
to / read

Review 02 pp. 46-47

A

Who
in / order / to
What
Why
Where

B

Who is it
me
in order to store food
What did you do
Why didn't you store any food
mine

Where shall I go

Unit 07
Grammar Exercise pp. 49-51

A

1. too / long / to / wear
2. too / tired / to / study
3. enough / to / lift

B

1. 너무 어려서 그 책을 이해할 수 없다
2. 너무 더러워서 마실 수 없다
3. 가장 윗선반에 닿을 수 있을 정도로 충분히 키가 크다

C

1. The bag is too heavy to carry.
2. This coat is big enough to wear.
3. The weather is too cold to go for a jog.
4. The hero was brave enough to save the girl.
5. Do you have enough time to finish the test?

D

1. so boring that I can't(cannot)
2. so tall that I can't(cannot)
3. so dirty that I couldn't(could not)
4. so sleepy that I couldn't(could not)

E

1. This paper is too difficult to use.
2. The camera was too expensive to buy.
3. The pot is too hot to touch.
4. The cheetah runs too fast to catch.

F

1. She is too young to go to school.
2. It was so cold that I couldn't go out.
3. He was too shy to talk to her.
4. They studied hard enough to pass the test.

Answer Key

Writing Practice pp. 52-53

A

1. Dan is kind enough to help poor people.
2. Tom was too nervous to sleep.
3. The weather was warm enough to go on a picnic.
4. The medicine is too bitter to take.
5. The sun is so far away that we can't visit it.
6. This painting is simple enough to understand.

B

1. These boxes are too heavy to handle /
   The mirror is so big that I can't move it
2. The zoo is exciting enough to visit /
   Some animals are too wild to feed

C

too / shy / to / say
kind OR friendly / enough / to / talk

Unit 08
Grammar Exercise pp. 55-57

A

1. places / visit
2. dream / be
3. problem / solve

B

1. to wear
2. to travel
3. to sit
4. to ask
5. to use

C

1. many poor people to help
2. some furniture to move
3. a book to return
4. a report to write
5. some vegetables to buy

D

1. 준비할 시간
2. 돌봐야 할 아이들
3. 심을 꽃씨들
4. 먹을 음식
5. 배드민턴을 칠 장소

E

1. He needs a phone to call.
2. They need a table to put in the kitchen.
3. She needs a sweater to wear.
4. We need friends to spend time together with.

F

1. I have some words to memorize.
2. Jean has some friends to visit.
3. They had several tables to set.
4. Peter needs a bike to ride to school.

Writing Practice p. 58-59

A

1. I found an interesting novel to read.
2. Did you buy the costume to wear on Halloween?
3. I have many things to do today.
4. This is the best time to visit England.
5. She had no money to spend. OR
   She didn't have any money to spend.
6. The children need an adult to help.

B

1. Julie wants someone to talk to(with) /
   Her teacher always has good advice to give

2. He had homework to do /
   his dad called a repairman to fix it

C

to / stay / healthy

to / work / out

not / to / eat

Unit 09
Grammar Exercise pp. 61-63

A

1. surprised / hear
2. proud / win
3. happy / meet

B

1. 이해하기 어렵다
2. 시작할 준비가 되어있다
3. 믿기 어려웠다
4. 대답하기 쉽지 않다

C

1. am glad to
2. am sorry to
3. is likely to
4. was disappointed to
5. were surprised to

D

1. ③ ① ②
2. ② ① ③
3. ③ ② ①
4. ① ③ ②
5. ② ① ③

E

1. Dan was glad to help the old people.
2. Many people are eager to learn English.
3. Jane is afraid to talk to strangers.
4. We are lucky to be alive after the earthquake.
5. Ben was sad to leave his family.

F

1. Bad habits are not easy to break.
2. I am happy to buy the book.
3. The wet floor is dangerous to walk on.
4. I am very sorry to bother you.

Writing Practice pp. 64-65

A

1. Your report is hard to understand.
2. We are disappointed to know the truth.
3. I am glad to join the school band.
4. He was angry to find the broken window.
5. Dorothy was surprised to see him at the door.
6. His dream is likely to come true.

B

1. I am proud to be a member of the speech club /
   I was afraid to speak in front of many people
2. He was surprised to hear the news /
   The news was hard to believe

C

was / sad / to

is / happy / to / meet

is / likely / to / spend

Review 03 pp. 66-67

A

to / talk

to / play / enough / to

to / help

enough / to

Answer Key

B

three things that I need most

a friend to talk with

friendly enough to listen to

need a pet to play with

lovely enough to relieve my stress

too busy to help

to help me with my homework

powerful enough to solve any difficult problems

be happy to have them

Unit 10
Grammar Exercise pp. 69-71

A

1. decided / buy
2. plans / go
3. want / get up

B

1. to be
2. to work
3. visiting
4. to finish
5. sharing

C

1. to buy
2. writing
3. to share
4. to move

D

1. ② ① ③
2. ① ③ ②
3. ② ① ③
4. ① ③ ②
5. ③ ② ①

E

1. to study
2. to send
3. closing
4. to go
5. reading

F

1. Becky wants to have dinner with us.
2. My sister decided to become a singer.
3. Jody tried to work out every day.
4. I could finish writing the report with his help.

Writing Practice pp. 72-73

A

1. I hope to meet you today.
2. He forgot to turn off the light.
3. Naomi promised to call her mom.
4. We decided to invite everyone to the party.
5. The two countries agreed to keep the peace.
6. Avoid speaking too much for a while.

B

1. I planned to go to the concert with my friends /
   I expect to see my favorite singer there
2. He always enjoys helping others /
   Kevin and I decided to do volunteer work
   together

C

plan / to / go

need / to / study

hope / to / have

Unit 11
Grammar Exercise pp. 75-77

A
1. encourages / finish
2. expect / come
3. allows / take

B
1. me to read
2. her friend to help
3. me not to forget
4. me to go out
5. him to be polite

C
1. 내가 식물에 물을 주기를
2. 그들에게 소란을 피우지 않도록
3. 우리에게 유니폼을 입도록
4. 그녀에게 너무 많은 사탕을 먹지 말라고
5. 내게 앉도록

D
1. to care
2. to get
3. to leave
4. to swim

E
1. Frank encouraged us not to lose hope.
2. They expected him not to skip class.
3. Vicky wants me not to waste time.
4. We told them not to take the bus.
5. I advised her not to drink too much soda.

F
1. My mom never forced us to eat food.
2. My parents don't allow me to stay out late.
3. Our teacher told us to recycle paper bags.
4. The doctor advised me to work out regularly.

Writing Practice pp. 78-79

A
1. I did not expect him to become a writer. OR
   I didn't expect him to become a writer.
2. She told me not to skip meals.
3. Banks encourage people to save money.
4. My mother wants us to drink milk.
5. She advised me not to play computer games.
6. We expected him not to run a race.

B
1. My mother wanted me to be(become) a scientist /
   She encouraged me to ask
2. He did not allow me to stay up late OR
   He didn't allow me to stay up late /
   He advised me not to eat too much fat

C
told / us / to / draw
allowed / us / to / use
advised / us / not / to

Unit 12
Grammar Exercise pp. 81-83

A
1. something / new
2. anything / cold
3. nothing / dangerous

B
1. anything sad
2. anything wrong
3. something delicious
4. nothing bad
5. something special

Answer Key

C

1. 멋지고 귀중한 (어떤) 것을
2. 부드러운 (어떤) 것을
3. 신나는(재미있는) 볼 것이 아무것도 없다
4. 달콤한 것은 (아무것도)
5. (무언가) 중요한 것이

D

1. anything
2. something
3. anything
4. nothing
5. something
6. nothing

E

1. I'm looking for something special.
2. There is nothing serious to worry about.
3. Some people should not eat anything sweet.
4. We found something funny in this photo.
5. She doesn't want to hear anything bad.

F

1. Pam wants to buy something different.
2. I don't see anything strange in this picture.
3. There was nothing fun in that game.
4. The little girl loves to have anything pink.

Writing Practice pp. 84-85

A

1. There is something wonderful in his magic. OR
   There's something wonderful in his magic.
2. I did not do anything wrong during the game. OR
   I didn't do anything wrong during the game.
3. There was nothing new in his invention.
4. My teacher wants something creative from me.
5. The old man taught us something important.
6. Something strange happened to him.

B

1. Veronica enjoys something challenging /
   Yesterday, I heard something unbelievable
2. Ray gave me something special last month /
   It became something important in my life

C

something / to / ride
something / delicious
anything / boring

Review 04 pp. 86-87

A

anything / scientific
to / invent / something / good
working / on / a / team

B

want to be a scientist
interested in anything scientific
to read science books
to invent something good for people
help people with it
working on a team
want to be a member
advises me to study hard

Unit 13
Grammar Exercise pp. 89-91

A

1. walked
2. shut
3. tried
4. changed
5. played

6. forgotten
7. dried
8. stopped
9. begun
10. thought
11. invented
12. given

B

1. baked / potatoes
2. painted / wall
3. closed / windows

C

1. updated
2. washed
3. respected
4. broken
5. printed

D

1. guided
2. stolen
3. injured
4. written

E

1. I always try to eat only cooked food.
2. Linda picked the fallen flower.
3. We need an upgraded version of this game.
4. Jack brought us a fixed radio.
5. Many people invited to the party didn't come.

F

1. The police arrived at the robbed bank.
2. The picture drawn by your sister looks good.
3. Some students prefer to buy used books.
4. There were not enough doctors for the wounded soldiers.

Writing Practice pp. 92-93

A

1. I am looking for my lost puppy. OR
   I'm looking for my lost puppy.
2. The towel left on the chair is mine.
3. She healed a bird with a broken wing.
4. Tina likes frozen yogurt as a dessert.
5. The police found the stolen car near the parking lot.
6. Alice opened the locked door with a big key.

B

1. I saw the boy hit by a car /
   the drunk driver caused the accident
2. My friend named Jody is very smart /
   she likes reading books written in German OR
   she likes to read books written in German

C

posted

talented / students

given / instructions

Unit 14

Grammar Exercise pp. 95-97

A

held / spoken / served

1. spoken
2. served
3. held

B

1. 수동
2. 능동
3. 수동
4. 수동
5. 능동

Answer Key

C

1. polluted
2. was caused
3. were taken
4. will announce
5. was baked

D

1. was born
2. be played
3. was blocked
4. was hosted

E

1. The essay was written by Tom.
2. His room was cleaned by Steven.
3. Many forests are destroyed by people.
4. The broken computer was fixed by my uncle.
5. The meeting was canceled by Henry yesterday.

F

1. The building wall was painted last week.
2. The thief was arrested by the police.
3. Cartoons are loved by many children.
4. The story was written by Dan a year ago.

Writing Practice pp. 98-99

A

1. The tickets were sold out in a moment.
2. These cucumbers were grown in the backyard.
3. The machine was fixed by Tim.
4. The cup was dropped on the floor by my brother.
5. Angela is loved by everybody.
6. This song is sung by many teenagers.

B

1. My bike was stolen by a thief a week ago /
   It was usually kept in the yard
2. English is spoken in many countries /
   Many famous books are written in English

C

be / built
will / be / changed
will / be / used

Unit 15
Grammar Exercise pp. 101-103

A

1. Nobody
2. anybody
3. Somebody

B

1. is
2. likes
3. Does
4. is
5. wants

C

1. Someone
2. anybody
3. No one
4. anybody
5. someone

D

1. 누군가 오늘 아침에 너에게 전화를 했다.
2. 누구든 열심히 노력한다면 성공할 수 있다.
3. 아무도 그 계획에 불평하지 않았다.
4. 누군가를 돕는 것은 너를 행복하게 할 것이다.
5. 아무도 그 파티에 오지 않았다.

E

1. Somebody OR Someone

2. anyone OR anybody

3. no one OR nobody

4. anyone OR anybody

F

1. Anybody can go to public school.
2. Somebody called while you were out.
3. There is somebody at the front door.
4. Nobody was brave enough to save the girl.

Writing Practice pp. 104-105

A

1. Somebody(Someone) should take care of the problem.
2. I didn't know anyone in this area.
3. No one is willing to take a risk.
4. Nobody knew he was a famous artist.
5. Anyone(Anybody) can understand the easy game.
6. I need someone(somebody) to explain this story.

B

1. I did not see anyone(anybody) there OR
   I didn't see anyone(anybody) there /
   There was nobody except some rats
2. I heard someone(somebody) calling my name OR
   I heard someone(somebody) call my name /
   I could not see anyone(anybody) anywhere OR
   I couldn't see anyone(anybody) anywhere

C

someone

anyone

someone / help / you

Review 05 pp. 106-107

A

is / broken

no / one

is / filled / with / nobody

B

in the classroom yesterday

closed

is broken

no one answers

is stained with ink

no one

is filled with scribbles

nobody will answer